It IS All about You

It IS All about You

A Responsible Search For Meaning

Dolah Saleh

BALBOA.
PRESS

A DIVISION OF HAY HOUSE

Balboa Press books may be ordered through booksellers or by contacting:

Balboa Press
A Division of Hay House
1663 Liberty Drive
Bloomington, IN 47403
www.balboapress.com
1 (877) 407-4847

Print information available on the last page.

ISBN: 978-1-9822-0047-3 (sc)
ISBN: 978-1-9822-0046-6 (hc)
ISBN: 978-1-9822-0048-0 (e)

Library of Congress Control Number: 2018903274

Balboa Press rev. date: 04/06/2018

Contents

Introduction

Our Stories

I had to ask myself: Why write about man's search for meaning? It's been done before. What's there to talk about? What more is there to say? We've got places to go, people to see, and life to live. These discussions don't really have much usefulness; they don't get us anywhere or make living any easier, do they? Interested audiences may be limited to the philosophical types, given to intellectual discussions for their own sakes. If we can never know the answers and it remains such an untenable matter, why bother?

The truth is that most of us—openly or secretly—want to engage and willingly enter into meaningful life discussions, whether we are in groups or one on one. My own undying investigative nature into the workings of man has brought me into countless conversations that begin with identifying a proper career path and inevitably fall into purposeful life reflections. In the course of my work with clients of great diversity, I've found myself in the same conversations over and over again. I am confident that I am not alone in this.

In fact, I have been having meaningful life conversations for as long as I can remember with, it seems, almost everyone. I figure that's why I was led into a career path where this interest—or need—might best be put to use. The experience that initiates my consulting contacts usually involves one of a job loss, one that my clients almost always highly regarded. They truly cared about it—or *thought* they did.

And so the story unfolds with great regularity. What begins as a search for a job morphs into a quest for purpose. The essence of inquiry is stimulated by a thought of whether one wants just another job, something to do for a living (i.e., work, better known as a euphemism for pain, something one has to do to pay bills and support a lifestyle), or that other thing in the back of one's mind, perhaps the new or renewed consideration more akin to something more personally meaningful, something the individual actually enjoys doing. Might we even dare ponder a calling, passion, or dharma, something one was meant to do? The individual wonders, *Is there such a thing for me?*

Some of the more enlightened among us believe that we enter this life having chosen our unique path, only we "forget." We have no conscious access to the memory. Our lives, if given us with predetermination and our consent—like a pact we make with our Source—serve as the vehicle to learning what we need in order to finally "get it right" and return home.

If this belief suggests reincarnation and lives lived in some sort of cumulative evolution of the spirit, it offers one explanation. It seems unlikely that we accomplish all our learning in the course of one lifetime. Even the revered scientist Albert Einstein believed that the past, present, and future happen all at the same time. That would mean that there is no separation; time is an illusion. But some concepts can be too obtuse to wrap our rational heads around.

The perpetual quests of humanity—those considerations we ponder and for which we seek the answers—sometimes begin when we are very young and continue on into old age, when we often become more philosophical. Here are the main ones:

Who am I (in this existence)?

Why am I here?

What should I and must I do;

        is there a *meant to do* for me?

What role do my relationships play?

Am I working with a predetermined time frame or life span?

What will it all mean in the end?

These questions reflect our need to know that our lives matter, that there is some reason for our being here. Somewhere we recognize that all our achievements and what we possess mean nothing. It's not that having "stuff" is bad; it's just *nothing*. We are not what we do or possess.

Even our most essential concerns attached to this earth cease to be. As we come to a close in this incarnation, our detachment must be a joy. In this brief "parenthesis in eternity," as self-help author Wayne Dyer called it, we do waste precious time in meaningless pursuits. Deep inside we know what truly matters. We do possess internal wisdom. Whether or not we do something about what we know; how long it will take us to act on this knowing—that's where choice enters in. The spiritual psychotherapy teaching in *A Course in Miracles* assures that we will get our intended curriculum no matter what, but we have choice in how we acquire the learning.

The first of the six major questions mentioned here (who am I?) is one of identity and degree of awareness. The second question (why am I here?) speaks to the issue of meaning, and the third (am I meant to do something particular in this time?) references the material manifestation of our purposes. The relationship question is one of necessity; our experience here involves others, each of whom we may encounter for various purposes and lengths of time. The duration of our finite stay is not known to us, but I have a hunch it is better this way. And the last question (What is the meaning of it all?) represents our unique karma, for in the end we may consider that our eyes come to see clearer and our ears to hear better; our hearts more whole and wide open, no longer bearing the breaks of our earlier experiences.

Many of us place our trust in religious affiliations and spiritual philosophies that adequately comfort us and allow us to quell these serious concerns for the most part. In contrast, if we are of the opinion that this is all there is, there wouldn't be much motivation to question our time here. Life would simply be as it is, and go as it goes, and one day simply come to an end. I suspect that those who think this way are either in the vast minority or covertly hold out the possibility that they may be wrong. Most of us get around to considering the notion of a meaningful life.

It might be that we need a picture, perhaps a storyboard or a yellow brick road, involving as many of the senses as possible.

We can be consummate procrastinators, especially while we are young. *There's always tomorrow.* It may be that we are too busy, distracted, or in denial. There is resistance in getting straight to the business of a conscious look at our responsibilities in our life's purposes. Some of us continue to view ourselves at the effect and not the cause of our lives. Does this mean we question it or misunderstand it or both?

In *The Unheard Cry for Meaning,* Viktor Frankl assures us that "someone worrying about the meaning of life is proving his humanness." He says the quest for meaning is not neurotic but rather a "distinctive characteristic of being human. No other animal has ever cared whether or not there is a meaning to life. But man does."

If you are one to believe that things happen to you and not *for* you, then please consider that you have both an opportunity and an invitation. There is benefit from our willingness to look, to see with eyes wide open. We can ask with the expectation of being properly guided. We can get quiet enough for long enough to hear the answers that reside deep within us.

This is not a book about answers but about the questions we all share. That's because you will not find answers on the pages of any book or in the words spoken or written by anyone else, no matter how wise you consider the "teacher." It is about a journey into your self because we were each born with the answers we seek. Consider that somehow in the human experience we have just forgotten our way; we've been led and misled, intentionally and unintentionally. Each of us gets to clear our own debris from the path of the stories we live.

Chapter 1

Who Are You? Being and Self-Awareness

All human beings are the same—made of human flesh, bones, and blood. We all want happiness and want to avoid suffering. Further, we have an equal right to be happy. In other words, it is important to realize our sameness as human beings.

—His Holiness, the Dalai Lama

I was fairly young when I began to form thoughts around the importance of knowing myself, yet the world around me did not seem to care about that. It was clear that the school curriculum had not been designed to instruct on any type of self-awareness or inner awareness, and my parents, although they made casual references, never addressed who I was or why I might consider a particular career path based on what I seemed to excel at or have interest in. And we might as well forget about discussions relative

1

to passion or "calling" and who I was at the deep soul level. There appeared to be no outlet for such investigation.

Given this backdrop, it is no wonder we are challenged by the notion of who we are, especially at a young age. Most of us have a sense of our day-to-day preferences, and we easily speak to those. But we consistently encounter people who easily admit that they do not know the direction in which they are meant to point themselves. They don't know what to choose for their personal and work lives, especially in order to live purposeful, meaningful lives. Is that not due to a lack of self-awareness? Most of us eventually feel the tug about a life that matters. After all, *what other kind of life is there?*

Confusion about the direction in which to point ourselves, whether personally or for meaningful work, is a definite indication that we are not in touch with our personal truths. When we know ourselves, there is a greater probability that we will honor our uniqueness and make decisions that support us and are consistent with who we are. It leads us to acknowledge our authentic selves and not be swayed or dissuaded into various detours. It saves us time and frustration.

When we heed our intuition, we touch that place within our deepest knowing; it will not mislead us. Moreover, the resulting self-acceptance gained naturally draws others to us in the same positive energy. It is literally the power of attraction, a symbiosis with the "right" people and commensurate career path. It doesn't matter what we call it. It can be self-confidence, self-acceptance, self-love, or even common sense. It is infectious and causes others to be drawn to us and be powerfully affected by us.

Our higher state of mind brings us an understanding of our oneness, ensuring there is no separation, but this is not to deny that we have form uniqueness to tempt us into believing otherwise. We certainly appear very different in myriad ways. That is why I wanted to address the idea that it is all about you— the expression of each individual and his or her business here— in the discovery of true identity as one within the collective consciousness.

The "Who am I?" question often is answered from the context of our relationship to others; how we are linked, such as daughter, sister, and friend. We may consider identity from our professions, such as teacher, engineer, or salesperson. We can use adjectives that describe our characters, such as helpful, loving, responsible, and restless. What we do for a living and how we are in relationship with others is important, and to some extent, through demonstration, it defines our internal guiding principles. They are a reflection of our preferences, ethics, and morals as members of the human race. But none of that is who we are.

The great awareness comes slowly, piece by piece.
The path of spiritual growth is a path of lifelong
learning.

—M. Scott Peck

An "Assessment Process"

By the time I meet clients, they are in the process of a coerced version of self-discovery, usually in midlife. They are delighted and receptive about gaining this often-clearer awareness and understanding of self through a personal-needs assessment process. Delivered in black-and-white, the reports often validate what they can no longer avoid, allowing for an experience that facilitates decision making. There is an opportunity to step back, often for the first time in their lives, and ask themselves important questions that get them behind their cover stories and onto a clear path of what makes unique sense for them. It brings the light into a type of darkness that was created as they moved subconsciously from one moment to the next in their lives. It brings hope into what may have become a mundane routine.

My clients, generally in full agreement with whatever the reports reveal about them and their motivational needs, see the benefits of a career (life) transition process. But they invariably ask questions that only could be considered entirely logical: "Why did I have to wait until midlife to sit with this beneficial information? Would this not have been wonderfully helpful to me when I was facing daunting decisions in my twenties or when I was graduating from high school?"

Today, there are a variety of aids to bring us into greater self-awareness and understanding. And indeed, it would be both logical and helpful to have this information and reflection time available to us as young as our late teen years, when we are expected to make choices that will affect our entire lives.

Living only on the surface of what is possible for us is no way to live, professionally or personally. This thought was a catalyst for me to pursue and fine-tune a career direction into the field of assessment. It became the passion that rose from an intent to help others in avoiding time spent unnecessarily in a place and space of poor fit. I resonate with a warning I once read in a book by Wayne Dyer—to not "die with [your] music still in you"—and I am circumspect. I can help others uncover the layers and barriers so they can come into their own greater awareness. In sharing what has been of benefit to me, I hope to reach and help others.

> Whatever limits the entrance of awareness limits healing.
>
> —Steven Levine

I can recall journaling once on the purpose of my life, and what surfaced was rather somber poetry. I look back today and see the melancholy there, but I wasn't hopeless; I just questioned everything!

We arrive to this planet with particular propensities. Mine was one of deep curiosity so that all I heard and was exposed to led me to self-inquiry, pushing me down certain roads and prodding me to get my attention. Then in my work, listening to people's stories, I began to recognize how most seemed to be in their "rightful" spots, even as they complained they were not, that they were unhappy and not where they wanted to be.

During my good moments, I help people see their places from a different light, from the place of intention. I encourage them to take a part of their lives with which they are pleased and draw connections, showing them how they could not have had the good parts had it not been for the other thing—the thing they didn't like so much. Other times, I trust they will eventually see how they were drawn in a particular direction, like a magnet, sometimes never understanding how or why until much later.

The push and pull of attraction for my own professional pursuits is no surprise, given what we know about teaching ourselves what we need to know for ourselves. The reason that I get attracted to the discovery of what motivates others is indicative of how desperate I am to look into my own needs, which drive me. And the only reason I want to know this and have the information confirmed in black-and-white is that it might otherwise be tempting to ignore (or deny), and I continue to live in a less-than-conscious state of mind—in other words, not self-aware.

For me, this translates to a life unfulfilled.

But my having more information about myself isn't quite enough. Perhaps it begins to trigger my deeper understanding, rather than merely providing data. The knowledge is there within me. I may have managed to subjugate this knowing to whatever surface matters took up temporary residence in the living of my life. But the good news is that I can make contact with it the minute I decide to do so, with a little willingness and trust.

So how can we uncover our truths and get to the business of living meaningful lives?

By paying attention.

Here is an example that comes from an experience I have had in numerous sessions with clients of all backgrounds and work statuses: There is "agreement" with the stated results, both on the self-reported portion of the assessment and what is revealed from the more obtuse "psychological" questioning. Even when people are working in jobs that have little to nothing to do with the stated revelations, they invariably acknowledge that they knew that but, for whatever reason, never allowed it to be the driving force in their lives.

Too many of us were not taught to heed our intuition. When we are still quite young, this "who we really are" eludes us, so how are we to be true to what we do not know or understand? Our sense about who we are is easily undermined by other factors, such as environmental influences, well-intentioned parental involvement, consequent financial and hierarchal goals (fame and fortune), etc., all significant in the material world. Once we mature, the possible incompatibility of internal happiness and external goals comes into clearer focus. Thus, we often decide in midlife or later life to pursue dreams left behind in the dust of our true identity and what we want to spend the rest of our time doing. Trusting in our ability to manage the transition is key, particularly against the backdrop of what we call our current lifestyle requirements.

Intuition is a sacred gift; intellect its faithful servant.

—Albert Einstein

In a 360 assessment process, there is an opportunity to involve others in evaluating us by their reporting on their perceptions of our behavior. Our peers, superiors, and subordinates are asked to respond to a number of questions, the results of which generate a consensus report that combines perceptions about the person being assessed. It is an important aspect, as it brings into our awareness how we are perceived by others, signaling how our behavior *affects* others.

Are the perceptions of those who work with us, befriend us, etc., accurate? Are they more accurate than our self-assessments or less so? Just as accurate? Attempts to reconcile the two is the theoretical objective of this process. The composite picture allows for a richer experience of self-awareness.

Others can help us uncover behaviors of which we remain unaware. The 360 process can highlight what we do that either contributes to or detracts from our environments. How we behave is a reflection of what is going on inside of us. If we feel positive, we tend to behave in ways consistent with that positivity. If we feel bad, our behavior is generally more negatively reflective. We can't get away with faking it, as there is cognitive dissonance—the idea that what we manifest is consistent with our beliefs, attitudes, thoughts, and feelings. There is consistency in the universe, or there is incongruence. But when we say or do that which is inconsistent with what we feel inside, our nonverbal messages give us away.

Even well-intentioned, intellectually oriented objectives can get in the way and obscure our vision into who we truly are. In the later high school years, we witness firsthand the effects on students with the overemphasis on prestigious universities and high SAT scores. We have to wonder, *Isn't anyone thinking of the individual child's heart?* Is no one willing to consider the most important element in decisions related to the pursuit of higher education? What if this child's calling is being totally ignored in this rote process of college selection and competitive scoring on standardized tests? And what real good is it to get in to the best school when that experience may entirely bypass what the heart says is true for the child and his or her purpose here?

Your opinion of me is none of my business.

—Mark Twain

I recently had a dream in which I felt that someone I knew well was judging me. In the dream, I was doing something that felt right to me, but in the eyes of my observer, it was an action that was being judged. I was a bit self-conscious, even as I experienced ambivalence, but remained in my choice and struggled with a precarious balance of self-assurance and falling for the criticism.

My realization, upon awakening, was that I have often allowed people's opinions of what I do and how I do it to have some sort of influence in my life. What causes me to believe that what someone else thinks of me and/or what I do is more important or more correct than what I think or know myself?

Upon closer examination, I see that it is a part of me that judged me, but the disguise is a convincing one. No one can do to me what I haven't done to myself first. It is a disconnected part of me but nevertheless alive and actively having a say as I go through my daily life. When I sit in judgment of myself, I see that reflected in the words and actions of others. I'm actively involved in projection. It is happening for me and my own self-awareness. What a beautiful wake-up call for me to see what I am doing to myself—that I buy into this idea of my being "not all right"!

Having not been willing to stand up for my truth has caused more trouble for me and others in my so-called field than it would have if I'd stood, clear and forthright, for what happens to be true and right for me. When we stand for something—whatever it is—we gain the respect reflected back to us in the eyes of others. When we are true to ourselves, we provoke that in others. But when we grant the wiggle room that comes with self-doubt, we fail ourselves and others. We lose our way.

When I want to make everything all right for everyone, even and especially at my own expense, it tells me that my thinking is flawed; I believe that other people have something I do not have! Fortunately, a shift can occur but may happen only when the pain of not changing becomes greater than the pain of changing.

In *A Course in Miracles*, we learn that all problems, no matter the form, come from fear. In my case, it was the idea that there was something wrong with me, and this self-judgment led me to do what was expected. This occurs frequently with young people in jobs or career path selection; it often happens in our pursuit of a personal mate and in the things we do or don't say and do. (*They* know better, so *I'd* better do that.) It can result only in our profound dissatisfaction because we fail to listen to our own reliable internal guidance.

I'm not speaking here of learning from the wisdom of those older and wiser than we are. There are always times we can benefit from those who have come before and wish to save us the trouble, even though we may need to experience most of it for ourselves. But to listen and act on the input of another to the exclusion of checking in with the self needs to be questioned. We gain much from paying close attention to the tugs of our own hearts. And as for those others with a strong desire to tell us what to do, attempts to obtain control—no matter how well intentioned—may have more to say about the imposer than of the one being led, taught, or imposed upon.

Herman Hesse eloquently addresses this in his famous book *Siddhartha* when he writes, "Which father, which teacher, could prevent [his child] from living his own life, from soiling himself with life, from loading himself with sin, from swallowing the bitter drink himself, from finding his own path?"

In another of my favorite books, M. Scott Peck's celebrated *The Road Less Traveled*, we encounter this same dynamic with reference to hand-me-down religion in his chapter on "Grace." He acknowledges that it is understandable that we inherit religious beliefs from our parents, but he cuts little slack in dismissing our responsibility later in life, when we have a chance to discover what works for us in our personal search for meaning.

My needing to please others is usually at the expense of my greater self-awareness. As time goes on, my true self gets hidden from my own understanding. It's been pushed down so deep that I don't even get to see it or sense it after a while. It is lost to me for a time—I am too preoccupied with distractions and a made-up fear of my own inadequacy. This acknowledgment was another not-so-surprising ingredient in my own decision to work at this business of assessment for identifying, uncovering, and clarifying motivational needs—first for myself and then for others.

I love the Mark Twain quote because it causes us to reflect on the fact that what someone says or thinks about us is nothing other than that—a thought expressed in the form of an opinion. And what we know about thoughts is that they are largely flawed because they are tethered to a problem rooted in the past. They mean nothing; they are disruptive and often mismanaged noise in our heads. When someone expresses an opinion aloud, that person merely is giving voice to nothing. It might as well be gibberish. The problem is that, for a time, *we think it means something*, and so now there are two people engaged in a dance of nonsense. This goes on routinely until we wake up to the truth that often comes in the form of laughter—our exit from angst. It is the release that can positively impact both giver and receiver simultaneously.

Recalling the quote also keeps me honest. When I am fortunate enough to catch myself giving my opinion (i.e., judgment), I have found it offers a splendid opportunity for a welcome moment of levity.

Generally, opinions of criticism originate in fear based thoughts of feeling either *not enough or better than*. What we know about superiority and inferiority complexes are that both signify questionable self-worth. These are more separation ideas that have no positive traction.

> There are three aspects of yourself to understand:
> That which moves, that through which it moves,
> and that which is the cause of the movement.
>
> —Swami Rama

Becoming self-aware with and through the help of feedback can be illustrated in simple, everyday examples. My sister once was speaking with our mother on the phone, and her roommate noticed that she was eating ice cream out of the container the entire time she was on the phone. After she hung up, her friend asked if she realized that she had consumed an entire pint of ice cream during the phone call. The friend added that it was something she had noticed before when (and, it seemed, *only when*) my sister was on the phone with our mother. My sister admittedly was taken by this observation. She had not been aware. That prompted her to consider the connection. Almost immediately, it was clear to her that the way she "tolerates" her resistance to Mother's call is to unconsciously engage in comfort behavior. This caused her unwanted weight gain and a subsequent feeling (reinforcement) of lower self-worth. It was an opportunity to make herself right again in her tendency to not value herself. The wake-up call allowed her an awareness of the compulsivity, offering her a more conscious choice to interrupt the undesirable behavior. There is often great power in simple awareness.

Other times it is more subtle. I once had a client who told me that he had begun dating someone new after his divorce, and sometime after the two became a couple, she told him that there were times she did not like the way he looked at her. He had to ask for more clarity because he had "no idea." She demonstrated what she meant and told him that it made her feel uncomfortable. What resulted was a shift to mindfulness that allowed him to manage himself; the couple is still together two years later.

The woman's comment had caused this gentleman to consider how he might have been in his marriage and perhaps with others, prior to this relationship. His awareness now is that when he has a thought, even if he speaks no words, it is expressed through a "look," thereby revealing his unconscious attitudes. What he corrected, he admits, was his thinking. Given the feedback, he was able to examine his thoughts, which essentially were faulty and led to self-sabotage. What he also realized was that those thoughts had nothing to do with the other person; they were coming from negative (and self-destructive) feelings that were attached to his past *regarding himself.*

There are times we experience a more transformational awareness. I had just turned thirty when my father died. A physician and family member had tried to quietly warn me that my father was "very critical." Looking back on it, I know that he was making a sincere effort to communicate the severity of my father's condition and was doing his best to prepare me for the inevitable. Still, when Papa died, I experienced incredible shock and was not at all prepared for his death. I was filled with regret and enormous pain. I came to recognize that during the time of my father's illness, I ran from my deepest feelings of sorrow. *If I refuse to look at it, maybe it will magically disappear.* Many years later, I identified with the words of one of my favorite authors—that we have to "look at what scares us" in order to conquer imagined fears.

For years, I recalled that period as a time when I was too young and incapable of being present to handle my emotions. We cannot and do not make reasonable decisions when we are emotionally absent to ourselves and others.

Recently, a dear friend was diagnosed with a serious condition. I was unable to control the swell of emotion on the day it was discovered, but I told myself that he would be fine. I would not believe in the seriousness; it simply could not be. He had licked a threat a few years earlier, and surely this would end similarly.

Later, my friend decided to enter into experimental treatment. Almost immediately, it was clear to me that I would not have elected a similar path, but rather than remain in authentic communication with him, I told myself to respect his wishes and to disregard my intuition. The truth is that I was so racked with my own fears—fear of what was happening, fear of losing him, fear of my own deepest sorrow—that it left me absent and ineffective. Here I was, so many years after I had done this with my father, running away again. I had not yet realize that attempting to avoid my fears was simply feeding them and causing me to behave in a manner that I would later regret.

If avoidance of our fears feeds them, then becoming aware of them would starve them to death. That alone ought to be reason enough for me to remain present, aware of what I am experiencing, and understand that my emotions are simply thoughts I am having. I am not my emotions. My thoughts have no power to hurt me, unless I insist on it.

> I might as well spend [my life] trying to look at what scares me instead of running away.
> —Pema Chodron, *When Things Fall Apart*

It has been a huge lesson for me. Being afraid to look at what amounts to mere thoughts has the power to hurt me and cause me tremendous pain. I have been presented with a creative variety of form circumstances in my life, providing me with numerous opportunities to manage the scary emotions; to acknowledge them, allowing them to be and then pass. We each have our unique forms of what we are here to learn.

The message even has come to me in the form of a dream. I have had a few different versions of a particular dream, in which I am having great difficulty opening my eyes. Often, I am at the wheel of a car or in some wildly frightening circumstance, where having "open eyes" or being able to see is critical. I am often brought to awakening, first in a panic and then in complete relief that it is not real. Thank God, I say, and then I explore the metaphor for what I need to see.

The dream is a short-lived play of form.

—Eckhart Tolle

Denial of our feelings, the unwillingness to experience what we feel—to acknowledge the pain rather than look away from it in some foolish attempt at self-protection—keeps us unconscious. That unconsciousness keeps us fearful and disconnected from the self.

Thankfully, our greater knowing is only buried alive and not gone forever. It is lying in wait, so we are able to dig it up with the forceful certainty and understanding that we aren't at the result but rather the *cause* for the circumstances in and of our lives. The choice is ours, and therefore we can choose differently the next time around, even with our thoughts—*especially* with our thoughts.

Moreover, the spiritual search is not about arriving at a particular point, where we now have something we did not have before or when we finally become something we are not.

Like Dorothy's experience in *The Wizard of Oz*, we have always had what we needed. This is what Michelangelo meant when he humbly responded to his admirers, assuring them that his incredible works of art merely were the result of removing the excess marble to find the beautiful structures within. *A Course in Miracles* refers to this as our job of removing "the blocks to the awareness of love's presence." It is the shaking off of our ignorance as we wake up to the truth of who we are. It is shifting from fear to love. That's how and where we reach God.

Most of us can identify a moment when we received (perceived) negative messages that had a great impact on our lives. There are times when it might have been done with negative intent, but usually these things happen in the most benign moments. For example, I can recall a time when I was perhaps eight or nine years old, and I was crying about feeling sad about something. My mom and others were nearby, and I made my way toward her, seeking comfort. What I recall is my mother's response to me as I placed my head on her chest. I soon felt her palm tap my back a few times as she excused me to those present. "Oh, my daughter—she's so sentimental." An immediate feeling inside me interpreted the back-tapping as a perfunctory response—dismissive and an indication that my mom was embarrassed by my behavior. The message for me was that to be "sentimental" was not a good thing. *Keep that stuff locked up.* No one wants to see *that*. I felt ashamed, causing me to erect a wall, one to shield me from ever experiencing that kind of discomfort again.

Today, I look back and recognize that the memory is there because of its fierce impact on me. In the presence of others, I held back my emotions, especially when I felt vulnerable. Who knows if my mother was aware and if she actually felt the way I understood it or even if it was possible that such an episode would be embarrassing (to her)? It could have been nothing more than a fabrication of my mind. What matters is that it was my interpretation that I lived and "died" with for many years, until I had an awareness that allowed me to let it go. It was the catalyst for repression and denial of my emotions, feelings that were running me even as I was not consciously aware of it.

No Accidents

You have heard this before: No matter what you happen to be doing right now, there is a reason for it, and it is not an accident. It is not a mistake, and there is no "if only ... then ..." about anything—not ever!

My career path took me from the field of education to business management to personal guidance/assessment to career-transition counseling to writing. I now see the common thread of these endeavors was seeking to know myself—my personal quest for meaning. Even when it looked like I was helping others to know themselves, I was led there because of my own self-interest in getting to know me.

It's the same for each of us. Isn't it great to know that we haven't wasted one second of our lives? In this way, we have done no wrong, no matter what it looks like. It is always only a matter of time, not substance. We can choose how long it will take us to get something, but the fact is that *we will get it*. The timing may be only and exactly when we are meant to get it—and not a moment sooner. Although the end may not seem to justify the means, it *will* tolerate it.

Gaining Clarity

What are the little questions behind the big ones? What do we ask of ourselves in an effort to get clear about our time here? The following are the questions that have seemed most prominently on the minds of those with whom I have engaged:

- Do I know who I am, and do I understand myself—what I like, why and how I like it, what my preferences and priorities are in a number of key life areas (family and relationship, career, spiritual, etc.)?
- How aware of and understanding am I about my own motivational needs as a driving force in my life?
- Have I been living my life in accordance with my values?
- Do I know that remaining in a less-than-aware state about my own needs will almost guarantee that I will be closed to the awareness of others in relationships, thereby resulting in less-than-authentic associations?
- Do I recognize that my decisions are often run by my

emotions, which are unconsciously attached to my thoughts that formed my attitudes and beliefs?

- Am I aware of how my behavior and my choices reflect my deepest feelings, not about others but about myself?

The unexamined life is not worth living.

—Socrates

On Emotion

The life path that I came to pursue brought more and more meaningful life resources my way. It often is said that when the student is ready, the teacher will appear. In the '90s, I happened to pick up another book that inspired me in ways I hadn't been up until then. The book, *Emotional Intelligence*, by Daniel Goleman, offered another piece of the puzzle into my examination of man and behavior (mine, mostly). Back then, it was almost the only book of its kind on the subject; it looked into a form of intelligence that may account more for our successes than its better-known form, intellectual intelligence. Emotional intelligence can be developed over time but not necessarily without conscious effort.

I did what I do with most books—I read it for the intellectual value and was able to incorporate it into my repertoire of knowledge. It was not enough to open my eyes, especially not enough to give me an experience of what I was up to with my own emotions. This work and the work I was doing in *A Course in Miracles* was about experience. How perfect; it was just the reinforcement support I needed—again!

Emotional Intelligence helped me to understand the motivation behind running away from my emotions/feelings. Moreover, it illuminated the fear of confronting something that was scary to me and apparently was *in* me. When I realized that it was only myself I was running from—that there was no bogeyman, no *thing* to fear—it lost its control over me, and I could take a closer look. I could sit with it and get to know it better, fully realizing that although feelings surface, they don't have to mean anything. They were not who I was. I wasn't the frightened guilty person that I felt like I was; I just experienced those emotions. Just becoming aware of this could dissipate the power it once had over me.

I read about how our feelings show us what we believe to be real and that emotions will take us to the absurd premises of our thinking—to the deceptions that we need to look into, those aspects to which we have been limiting ourselves. At first, I considered it very sad. Then I understood that even what I deemed "sad" was only a thought I had.

I practiced acknowledging my emotions, which brought me to the next level, where I could experience the relief that came with facing them. Inspirational Buddhist teacher Pema Chodron refers to this as "compassionate abiding." I could see that my interpretation was only imagined, not a reality. It stood in the way of my fully living in the light of my own life and truth. If that sounds a bit high-reaching, you may have yet to discover it for yourself without a whole lot of effort and much to gain.

> Only in an open, nonjudgmental space can we acknowledge what we are feeling. Only in an open space where we're not all caught up in our own version of reality can we see and hear and feel who others really are, which allows us to be with them and communicate with them properly.
>
> —Pema Chodron

In studying the dimensions of emotional intelligence, I saw that I hadn't been paying attention to my own feelings. We can't pay attention to what we are so busy running from. If we could personify our fears, what would they look like? Talk to them; ask them questions. The answers come. One practitioner of emotional intelligence asked participants to "try on" the feeling (or reaction) that they had, sit with it awhile, and see what occurred. When we are able to discern the difference between identifying with the emotion and simply seeing it as something that's passing through, it dismantles the fear, enabling denial to take a back seat. There is no longer any reason for it.

We can do something productive with our fear, such as befriend it, or have compassion for it, or laugh with it. We won't need to run from it because we recognize it as our creation— what we have, not who we are. We understand that our emotions mostly are connected to a past memory and therefore are a source of information. They have no credence other than to signal that at one time in our own history, an event became associated with a response that we continue to live with and react from and reenact over and over. Wow!

We see that we are being run by something that we do not even consciously acknowledge as a working present force in our lives. We see that something is controlling us that would otherwise be rendered impotent if we would *just take a look*!

Emotional intelligence discourages our inquiry into the *why* behind our feelings. It is about experience, not analysis. Instead, we are to observe and allow the inevitable insight to arrive. In my own inimitable fashion of wanting to understand it intellectually, I analyzed and was sometimes even able to glean enough information to help me in uncovering the cause behind my particular issue. But that did not help me change anything, even given its valiant attempt to pry open these eyes of mine.

Analysis with interpretation can end up perpetuating the toggle from guilt to blame. That's why therapy can be of questionable value; in the end, what we want is release, not explanation. Remaining hell-bent on interpreting our feelings won't help to uncover their true meaning—the wealth of what they are here to tell us. Our stories about the whys and wherefores often serve as delay tactics. If therapy fails to help us reach beyond explanation and see the promise and release of responsibility, it is of little use. On the other hand, experiencing the emotion opens us to seeing the difference between being it and having it.

I am easily the poster child for analyzation and interpretation.

I have spent countless hours dissecting every last nuance of behavior and action and nonaction. I have not been helped by this obsession. I only experienced relief once I finally allowed each emotion to come and go without making it mean something. This is the exact reason why some choose meditation as a way out. As they go quietly inside, they let go of each thought in the recognition that those thoughts are creations of an attached and busy mind and are absolutely meaningless.

When I first learned about the power of our emotions and how they could run us in unconscious submission, I felt like I finally understood something that previously had escaped me. I was relieved, as if knowing that it had a name cleared a path for me to change what was not working in my life. That's what conscious awareness does. It dismantles our autopilot of reaction and serves to bring us from unconscious reaction into conscious intention, where choice is facilitated.

It is important to note that there is a positive correlation between self-awareness and success. When we own, know, and accept ourselves, we are more likely to choose appropriately and live lives that makes sense for us. We experience a greater potential for happiness. At the other end of the spectrum, our failure to do that which we love or are intended to do makes it more likely that we will have a less-than-successful experience.

Results gleaned from a variety of personal needs assessments and feedback on emotional data allow for consideration and are resources that enable us to reach beyond the surface into our depths to explore possibilities. We run so fast in our daily lives, flitting from one person, place, or thing to another, that it is entirely possible we do not take the opportunity to stop and reflect. *What do I feel about this? How am I thinking here? What is going on for me in this moment?* There is an opportunity to question what we have been up to in a way that opens a door, one that invites us into our deeply private selves yet is our connection to everything in the universe.

We undoubtedly miss critical details when we don't truly know ourselves. In my experience there are too many of us who not only remain largely unaware of what is motivating us but who are unconscious of the emotional pathways that persist in our reactions. *What we are unaware of has control over us.*

Most of us have had the experience when, after a rather dramatic exchange, we question rhetorically, *what was I thinking?* We simply cannot believe or quite explain what just occurred because mere moments later, it seems unreasonable or even "crazy." The truth is that in those moments, *we are not thinking.* Our rational brain was disengaged by a part of our brain that is designed to save us from disaster. In that emotionally reactive state, logic or rational thinking is not available to us.

> We do the big escape: we act out, say something, slam a door, hit someone, or throw a pot as a way of not facing what's happening in our hearts. Or we shove the feelings under and somehow deaden the pain. We can spend our whole lives escaping from the monsters of our minds.

—Pema Chodron

The best thing about our EQ (emotional quotient) is that unlike IQ, which tends to be static throughout life, emotional intelligence can be developed. It behooves us to gain understanding as to where we fall on the emotional intelligence domains and learn what each can teach us about living more authentically and self-respectfully, thereby in a greater space of peace and contentment.

The results of such assessments can help us shine a light on something that historically has been kept in the dark. We might actually see that what we cannot forgive in another is what we cannot forgive in ourselves. What a great learning!

I am consistently drawn to the wonderful allegory of *The Wizard of Oz*. Having held a long-time admiration for the metaphors offered in the fable, I believe that it represents our search, our longing, and ultimately our coming into ourselves. It sounds simple to say that all it takes to be able to see (and make the shift) is a little willingness, but, as with Dorothy, it takes some courage to want to see and take our heads out of the sand. Once we do, wisdom may enter and motivate us to follow our hearts. But first we will be fooled into traveling down roads we never had to travel, encountering troubles we could have avoided, and projecting aspects onto people (in our dreams) that are mere reflections of our faulty thinking. A little willingness will take courage (to trust), wisdom (to learn), and heart (to be open to the love that was always there).

As the hope of a powerful wizard who has all the answers for us is shattered, we begin to realize that there is nothing out there in the world that can help us. We need to help ourselves, and the good news is that we have always had what we needed to accomplish that. Just as Glinda reassured Dorothy in the symbolism of the glittery red slippers, we *just thought we didn't have what it takes*. We fell asleep for a while and had a dream, but we can wake up now.

The experience of negative effects in our lives may only be there as long as we remain "asleep at the wheel," as my own dream showed me. With my refusing to look, I was essentially denying what I needed to see, which brought unappealing consequences. Once I decided to open my eyes and wake up, results were immediately evident and positively experienced. None of us needs to wait any longer to achieve that kind of realization. Our willingness to see allows us to avoid our cover stories that cause all the problematic delays. Although it looks as if each of us has a creative expression of what it is we uniquely need to know, the truth is it's all just one thing: that each of us is whole, a wonderful expression of love connected to and united with our Source.

We have all sorts of delay tactics and some are so creatively disguised it is a challenge to see that we are avoiding the inevitable. While it's true that we can take all the time we want, our understanding of how we can free ourselves of the burden of avoidance could help. We might not want to waste another moment in getting to live authentically right now.

By becoming aware of how we do this silly thing again and again because we don't want to dwell in the uncertainty and awkwardness and pain of not knowing, we begin to develop true compassion for ourselves and everyone else, because we see what happens and how we react when things fall apart.

—Pema Chodron, *When Things Fall Apart*

Chapter 2

Why Are You Here? Intention/ Reason for Being

Oh, we just get one ride around the sun,
In this dream of time.
It goes so fast that one day we look back,
And we ask, was that my life?
—Jo Dee Messina, "Was That My Life?"

You are a stranger in a strange universe. As you are catapulted onto the earth's stage, what are your desires? Where might you want to go? What will you want to do? What sorts of things do you want to have? Who do you want to *be*?

Right out of the womb, we are needy, wanting, and, to some extent, that continues throughout our lives. We are an attached people. It is the stuff of drama in the realm of theater and movies. What we want and what gets in the way of what we want forms the basis of plot theory and storytelling. Real-life stories provide ideal inspiration for interesting dramatization, and truth is often stranger than fiction.

So what drives our wants? The first thing we understand is that *to want* implies that we do not have—or at least we do not believe we have it; that's why we want it. Usually, the object of our intention is material, tangible. The other inference is that once obtained, we expect a certain level of satisfaction or even happiness.

Let's say that someone decides he wants a red Audi TT. He does what he needs to do, which might include working hard, saving money, obtaining a good credit rating, and then successfully arranging for the necessary combination of cash and financing. He gets his red Audi and realizes the direct correlation of his desire with his goal. He got what he wanted. At least for the moment, he is happy.

Now he has the car of his dreams; he feels great and accomplished. One day as he is traveling in his Audi, someone suddenly cuts him off in traffic and demolishes his beautiful possession, seriously injuring him in the process. Now what is it that he wants? Other than turning back the hands of time so that accident does not occur, he now likely has experienced a conscious shift in his priorities and wants to be physically whole and well again more than anything else. Still, in more of a psychological reconsideration, did he somehow manage to bring that humbling accident on to give him what he "really" wants? Did he *need* the Audi and the accident for some reason? Might that reason include shining a light on coaxing him to the realization of his true priorities? In this new moment, has the object of his desire shifted from a car to his well-being?

Naturally, we all know that without our health, little else matters. While this example sounds a little outlandish, most of us can think of a similar example, where someone got something she wanted, only to experience it as not very important, or getting what she wanted led to getting what she needed. As the saying goes, "Be careful what you wish for." The point is, what is the desire behind the desire? Is there a force behind the scenes at work to get us what we need, rather than what we think we want?

As we go along creating the circumstances of our lives, we do get exactly what we want, even if we fail to recognize it as such. We are not always consciously aware of our motivations— and likewise our feelings, attitudes, beliefs, or thoughts *behind* our behavior. It can all be quite hidden from us. So we are just humming along the trails of our lives, only to stumble upon a result that we may not have expected or desired—until, perhaps, we are willing to investigate in a manner that uncovers all the layers of unconsciousness with which we have been living.

> We either make ourselves miserable or we make ourselves strong. The amount of work is the same.
>
> —Carlos Castaneda,
> Journey to Ixtlan: The Lessons of Don Juan

When we take a close look at the topic of human longing, we see trends. There is our age-related wanting, such as money, status, and power, while we're still young. Then, as we grow older, our health consciousness may increase; we want good or better health and realize that we may no longer be able to take our physical well-being for granted. We want relationships, usually of various kinds, such as friendships and love. We want those relationships to be functional. We don't want them to be too much work. Sometimes we want to grow our own families and have children. Many of us have a longing for a spiritual connection in our lives. We also want and recognize the benefits of attaining more elusive qualities, such as happiness, peace, and joy.

Other times we hear people express that they "want to be" something in particular, such as a good person or wanting to be loved, appreciated, respected, and so forth.

Ultimately, there tends to be an awful lot of wanting in our lives. We want to go places and experience things, and we want long lives without too many challenges. We even want *not* to want for anything. Some of us concede that we need to settle and be reasonable; no one can have it all, right?

I had a friend who once spoke apologetically about his life thus far, at age fortysomething. He recounted his worldly successes but sadly admitted that he had failed to achieve what he deemed "personal success." When I asked him what he meant by that, he said that he was disconnected from his wife. While he took responsibility, he felt she was never the "right one"; there was no "fixing" it. He was convinced that his only chance was to start over. He meant with another person, someone with whom he could begin again in mutual love and support. That was his

34

newest desire. He was certain that his fear of being alone was the catalyst that kept him in his unhappy situation for twenty years, but he no longer had that fear. He would rather be alone than be with the "wrong person" again.

I was astonished at my friend's fatalistic attitude and alarmed by his seeming despair and depression when we spoke about this. He did not see that his behavior was a reflection of his own thinking and not because he and his wife were incompatible or because he needed someone with whom he had a more "ideal" connection. His relationship was exactly what he "wanted" to bring him back into his own connection with himself. If he misses that somehow, he is bound to repeat the experience with another, someone who has a different face but a comparable dynamic to incite a similar presentation for his benefit. In other words, he will experience the same content in different form. He will repeat this pattern until he gets that his life is the outcome of his own doing.

The Desire for God

My Islamic father questioned my religious beliefs in my youth. He asked me, "What do you do in church? Do you pray? Do you talk to the statues? What do you ask for? Do you say 'Oh, God, give me what I want. Give me what I need'?"

I didn't make much of those exchanges with my father at the time. I heard his sarcasm and recognized that he was trying, in his own little way, to convince his naive daughter that this wanting from God was the stuff of misguided belief. His interpretation of my Catholic God was pointed out in the silliness of concrete statues. His God, Allah, was "only One" and not represented in any form, concrete or otherwise. I considered that he was urging me to think clearly through this thing I was doing—this practice called Christianity.

Forget that we want there to be a Creator. Much of the time we are engaged in some expression of wanting from whom we deem our God. We direct our prayers and our requests to our Source to fulfill our earthly needs and desires. But if this Creator knows who we are, if our God really knows his creations, then this same being knows that we need nothing because we are made in the likeness of the perfection from which we came. So if we feel that God's not listening, maybe it's because he does not relate to our wanting. He or she knows we have everything we need.

Initially, this realization can sound a bit unfortunate. Do I mean we can't rely on our quiet moments with God to ask for what we want and need, with the idea of achieving some level of tangible satisfaction? I understood why ignorance is truly bliss. When someone of authority, such as a parent, hands you a belief, you go with it. It seems fair to have a foundation, one in which there seems to be a moral code by which to live, a non-secular system for reinforcing the legal and ethical codes of society. The consistency appears to be reasonable and good and designed to keep us in line and responsible. Furthermore, it is comforting to feel that there is some reward for being good, that we get to have things and enjoy ourselves when we ask and receive. A fair exchange, right? And let's not forget the desire for our ultimate reward in heaven for eternity.

Our beliefs can be brought into serious question and then perhaps entirely dismantled. For me, the idea of wanting God to grant me things was nothing to let go of compared to the angst of reconciling a God who is all-loving and all-forgiving but at the same time a punishing, angry God who watches my every move and will *get me* in the end. I never understood that, nor do I see how a God who loves me unconditionally could ever be angry enough at me to hurt me or judge me. Those appear to be entirely incompatible thoughts. I felt gently coerced into a greater consciousness and to initiate a search for another path to God because the chasm was getting bigger.

After reading countless self-help books and materials, I finally ended up with a not-so-little blue book titled *A Course in Miracles,* and I began to attend group sessions that brought me into a clearer understanding. It felt right. I met extraordinary people and did feel that I'd found something that resonated with me. The fact that Jesus happened to use a research psychologist from Columbia University as the scribe and that the learning contained so much of what I came to understand during my own studies in psychology made it ever more attractive to me. But now I was certain that there was no big guy in the sky who, if I asked and was good enough, would grant my requests. I realized that all this time, as silly as it might sound, I had envisioned a loving, older Supreme Being—a male, my divine Father. When I prayed, I had a face. I imagined him speaking to me and the conversations we would have.

And now, I could do that no longer. I know that we are all spirits, having a human experience, and that we are all one consciousness, even as it appears otherwise. We share the sonship *with* Jesus, our brother, part of the collective. Not only in the way that we are one as equals, but we are truly one having a dream. The truth is that only love is real; the rest, even thinking that we live on this planet, is illusion. It's an illusion conceived because we think we've separated from our Creator (and one another). In truth, the separation never occurred. Now it makes sense that we are the creators of our own dreams and sometimes live nightmares of our own making.

If Creator and Creation Are One

It may be that the one sustainable factor in my Catholic upbringing was the teaching that there are three persons in one God: the Father, the Son, and the Holy Spirit. Today, I do not have a personalized view of this Trinity; I have an integrated view with the universe in all lives living and seemingly once lived. For me, there are not only three persons in one God but the numerous manifestations that seem to appear over time—humanity itself, all rolled into oneness with our Source.

I was speaking to a couple of colleagues and spiritual seekers about beliefs, and we were getting all balled up in semantics, which often happens because words are somehow inadequate, limited in their ability to capture what is being communicated. All of a sudden, I expressed the frustration I felt: "It's not about beliefs, really, is it? It is *beyond belief*; it's about knowing!" All of us agreed and happily concluded that this beingness that we are, this truth that only love is real, is not so much what we believe but what we choose to know. We uncover this knowing once we strip away all the garbage that we've layered on in our state of perceived separation.

If we fall for a lesser idea of ourselves, we end up creating a methodology for coping. But who really wants to go through time simply getting from one challenging moment to the next? And the worst part is that we seem unable to do it alone; we need to recruit others to be in the muck right along with us, and so we drag and coax them in. Before we know it, there are a whole lot of us engaged in a very strange dance of unhappiness and dread.

Often it is within our various religious structures that many of us find a resource for coping and perhaps a type of resolution to the question of our time here. The desire opens us to being led and shown a way. The system is an anointed one, intended to give us what we think we're looking for. The system itself, however, is limited. We can take all the time we like in accepting our own power to choose responsibility for ourselves, or we can get to it right now.

Attachment, Dependence, and Addiction

All that we are attached to and depend on to make us happy and fulfilled sets the stage for what we come to want. I want money, position, power, and things, and I will do what I have to do in order to obtain and retain them, even if sometimes I do this at great cost.

In the meantime, it will look good and seem fine, even though it may not always *feel* good. Remember that our feelings are accurate barometers of the thoughts that created them.

Our pursuits become obsessive and distracting. They can sidetrack us from the real love for which we long. *A Course in Miracles* tells us that our jobs are to remove the blocks to the awareness of love's presence, not create more blocks. Real love needs nothing; it wants nothing. In a frantic acquisition mode, our truth is diminished. We attend to what does not matter.

Arriving at our classroom called planet Earth, we gain the lessons for which we came. We see with the body's eyes and live our lessons in the experience of the world stage. Along the way, we move toward the eternal peace, love, and happiness that is our birthright. Like Dorothy in *The Wizard of Oz*, rather than get right to the power of our Source, we take the more difficult and lengthy path. *A Course in Miracles* assures us that (just like Dorothy) we're already home; it just doesn't look that way.

Many spiritual leaders either hint at or directly state the idea that some of us are actually addicted to feeling bad. If that sounds strange, consider the child of an abusive home. When given a choice to leave, the child most often will prefer to remain. Why? Because the devil he knows is preferable to the devil he doesn't know. Familiarity wins out over the fear of the unknown. That's what happens when we become obsessed and addicted to what is not positive. We prefer to remain in the "as is" state, frozen with the fear of what is unfamiliar yet is our salvation.

I once knew a man who spoke very sincerely about his desire

to be an honest man. He was eloquent in the way he expressed that he enjoyed material success yet felt he'd failed miserably in the way in which he obtained this success. It was time, he said, to make that right.

Initially, he began by remitting anonymous "payback gifts" to those he either stole from or felt he had offended; he wrote letters of apology and truly appeared contrite and sincere in his desire to make amends.

But soon the unproductive behavior returned, belying his stated intentions. Those of us in his field experienced the incongruity. I particularly noticed that he operated in a less-than-conscious state most of the time and that he behaved in a reactive mode, generally speaking, rather than in a thoughtful, proactive manner.

There were times when this man expressed great thoughtfulness and consideration, love, and even patience. His challenge was that he was triggered so easily and quickly because his default (autopilot) rested heavily with some notion of diminishment. It was home base for him. He never believed himself to be the wonder that he truly was, and so his thoughts tended to sabotage his behavior, and his behavior belied his greatness.

We might ask of this man's situation: Did he really desire to turn it around, or was there a deeper need to cause himself greater pain and guilt to coerce himself into the readiness and willingness required to make a shift?

Perhaps this man's desire only reflected the wanting but in

the end was inadequate to move into becoming a reality for him. Desire is not yet intention, and so the wanting suggests the underlying belief that he doesn't have what it takes; he will not have it, and that's why it is stagnant. Seems strange, but this is an important distinction. Such an awareness, once assimilated, has the power to move him directly from wanting to having—in an instant!

> The privilege of a lifetime is being who you are.
>
> —Joseph Campbell

The real problem for most of us, when we say we want to be, is that we don't always understand that there is nothing other than ourselves in the way. Our state of being is our choice, our privilege, and ours alone to own. I believe my example shows a man 100 percent sincere in his wanting to be honest and whole, but he was unconsciously tied to a compulsive justification, caused by the lack of love he felt. He brought past times of dependency and disappointment into his present moment, making those perceived offenses real all over again. They played out just as he expected and, in fact, dictated. His fear ran him, rather than his expressed desire.

Assessment

We know we are born with clean slates. Beginning in the womb, we do receive messages from the environment into which we will emerge. But essentially, once here, the real learning begins. During those first three to five years, what happens to us is crucial in augmenting the blueprint that inevitably establishes our autopilot. Some of it is beneficial to us and others in our fields; other experiences are harmful and destructive to us and our environment. Lots of those more negative pathways will dominate and cause problems, not the least of which is a negative self-image. In terms of how it manifests behaviorally, psychiatrist and best-selling author M. Scott Peck once addressed this as a tendency to either take it out on ourselves (neurotics) or on others (character-disordered).

Remember that much of the cause for behavior gets buried. A professional assessment (such as with Emotional Intelligence) offers an ideal benefit to help uncover what is running us. The awareness we gain can expose some of the underlying causes that help us understand and then figure a way out of being driven by them.

The goal in the motivational needs assessment process is more about identifying what we need in order to achieve happiness and success. There is a clear benefit to engaging in a non-judgmental process that identifies what motivates us and what we need from our environment. Based on the results of our responses to a questionnaire and the reports generated, we get to understand both how we appear to others and what we feel inside. And to the extent that those are different, we gain awareness on how well or how badly we might be understood by others. That clarity opens the door for us to accept and embrace our own uniqueness. As a side benefit, it facilitates and improves our sensitivity to others' differences. These kind and loving shifts are powerful enough to change our worlds.

I remember hosting a career day when I was teaching sixth grade. This was a school invitation that went out to parents and others in the community to address students on what they did for a living. It was intended to provide young people with exposure to various professions and lines of work, as well as an opportunity to ask questions of the presenters, ostensibly to ascertain interest levels toward a particular career.

Perhaps I don't need to tell you that the children's queries largely demonstrated an inordinate amount of attention to the income and status level of these professions. It was fame and fortune that was of interest, rather than how these adults may have contributed to society in their respective roles. To say it was alarming is a bit of an overstatement, given what we know about the desire for or admiration of status, position, and celebrity in our society.

Most parents recognize how quickly their children reflect what they see and hear at home and with their exposure to the media. We know that there is a direct correlation with children's environmental experience and what they come to want for themselves. Over time, that orientation can range from an attachment on one end to obsession on the other. That is one reason why parenting is one of the toughest jobs on earth—if you get it too wrong, the consequences can be grave.

Our words and actions scream so loud that our children can't hear what we want for them in our hearts. I ask parents what they wish for their children, and they routinely respond that they want them to be happy. I believe them. But then, I hear judgments about other people's children, referring to them as "losers," saying that they're "going nowhere"—messages not lost on their children. Espousing our acceptance of whatever it takes to have our children experience happiness at the same time we place qualifiers and limitations on certain choices exposes blatant inconsistencies.

It is a similar inconsistency when parents are driving leased high-end vehicles and wearing designer labels, living in homes they can barely afford, and pursuing lifestyles that exceed their financial limitations. They insist on private education for their children so that they can rub noses with the upper crust in society, as if to suggest that on their own, they are not enough.

Where we want to end up, so to speak, will, to some degree, depend on what we value. What we know is that these are values that come from conscious and unconscious desires. Parents truly need to see their hands in how they create these desires for their children.

I remember the first time a dear friend of mine admitted she had no idea whatsoever what she intended for herself. I asked her why she had done this or that—rather substantial things, like relationships and jobs, which we agreed gave the impression that these choices were deliberate, well-thought-out, desired commitments. She admitted reluctantly that her choices were made with very little consciousness. She had simply done what she felt would get her what she wanted for the moment. It seemed like a good idea, given the time, but almost as soon as she reached a goal, it left her empty and wanting more—though more of what, she did not know. She sought continual comfort in people, places, and things, and I could see there was no comfort in any of that. After the initial high, it was back to the pursuit of another *some thing.*

My father used to remind me to consider what I needed versus what I thought I wanted. I hated being confronted with that because I thought they were the same. But we know they are often not the same. That's why being in touch with a values list that we thoughtfully gather and then looking at what drives us—our unique needs—is a very useful and worthwhile exercise, even without the benefit of professional assessment. Forget what you think you want, and pay kind attention to what you need. Develop a plan to achieve that for yourself. This creates intention that gets you closer to your true purpose.

Ultimately, the assessment process offers a deeper dive into what we need from our environments in order to achieve happiness and success. Maybe the reports help uncover the fact that whatever we have wanted has failed to serve us and our higher needs. When we meet our needs, we avoid wasted time and get right to the business of attending to what matters.

Until we are somehow brought into awareness, with the assistance of a feedback mechanism, we often engage in unconscious decision making. It's like trying to get somewhere we've not been before by just jumping in the car and going for a drive. The assessment offers the help we need to answer the questions of our authentic, meaningful desires and our purpose for being here.

Setting Goals

We are greatly familiar with the idea of setting goals in achieving our desires. If we want to get somewhere, we need to have a plan. I love the title of another of my favorite books: David Campbell's *If You Don't Know Where You're Going, You'll Probably End Up Somewhere Else*. We need measurable objectives to state our intended aim, accumulate that which is necessary to achieve the steps we identify, and then take action in the doing of those things. Those action steps move the goal forward, and then— presto!—we will *be* that which we set out to become.

That is indeed how many of us go about setting goals and measurable objectives. As we observe success, however, that is not what happens. In fact, this system is backward. Success is achieved by individuals who have first made a decision to *be* a particular way and who have the self-awareness that they are that. The foundation is accomplished in the being. Like everything, it starts with a thought. Actions—what they do—comes out of the being. It is a natural outcome. Finally, they attract into their lives accordingly. In other words, they *have* the object of their desires. As we understand the power of attraction, this is the way it works, optimally. We are being it first and doing what is consistent with that being. As a consequence, we attract what we want to have as a natural outcome.

The be/do/have way assumes the position that the actions that we take—and therefore the results that we achieve—are a reflection of who we know ourselves to *be*. As we pursue our dreams, they are powered by the reflection of who we are, in the highest honor and self-respect possible.

In Buddhist Thinking, Wanting Is Attachment

One of my very favorite idioms is this: "Be attached to nothing and accepting of everything." If we lived that way, I feel we would have a contented existence such that nothing could rattle us. Think about it. I want nothing and expect nothing, and whatever seems to be or happens, I remain nonresistant in my acceptance of what is. Just writing that makes me sigh with relief.

I love the story of *Don Quixote, Man of La Mancha*. He knows who he is and acts from that, irrespective of his detractors—those who poke fun and think he is out of his mind. In each step, his actions simply follow his being, which is a reflection of love, light, and beauty. Even though he is an object of criticism, he is impervious to opinions; they can't dissuade him because he is not attached to their opinions. He is also rather accepting of both himself and whatever others express. He has what he wants.

The spiritual journey does not consist of arriving at a new destination, where a person gains what he did not have or becomes what he is not. It consists of the dissipation of our own ignorance concerning self and life and the gradual growth of an understanding that begins the spiritual awakening. The finding of God is a coming into one's self.

Chapter 3

The Doing in Living

It is not enough to be compassionate; we must act.

—the Dalai Lama

Nothing in the world is worth having or worth doing unless it means effort, pain, difficulty ... I have never in my life envied a human being who led an easy life. I have envied a great many people who led difficult lives and led them well.

—Theodore Roosevelt

After we consider who we are and what we want here, we take action according to some version of our identities and intentions. Consider the daily experience of our lives; what does it look like? The question is, how do we make life choices? What are we doing as we're being?

Are we awake and aware so that what we do is reflective of

a life that has purpose and meaning? Or do we choose to spend our time fumbling around in the dark, stumbling and continuing in such a manner until a more serious message strikes us and forces us to wake up? There are many roads to Rome, and there is no doubt we will get there, but the question is, which route shall we take? Will it be direct or circuitous? How long and what time frames or lifetimes will we require? Do we choose the most expedient or one that could involve painful detours?

A *Course in Miracles* tells us that Jesus said we need do nothing. I have personally struggled with this, as I am quite a doer. I do a lot. No matter how hard I attempt to avoid spending day after day in a too-busy mode, I gleefully tick off one and then another item on my ambitious to-do list. It's my modus operandi. And while I also attempt to use what I understand about time management and try to get to those less-appealing tasks first, it is more often that I get to them last, but I do get there. *I have* to.

Actually, Jesus was referring to the broader truth that we are already home with our Creator. But for our purposes, we live in the illusions of our making, only thinking we need to take action and thinking we have needs at all. We have an identity and corresponding desires dictated by that identity. From the minute we can walk, we are off and running, going from one action to the next, doing all there is to do in our work and play.

Our challenge is the restriction of time. Each day's hours seem inadequate for all I need to get done. Somehow I suspect that I may be creating a distraction with my to-do list. I may choose this busyness as an avoidance tactic.

I wonder what I'm avoiding. Am I running away from me and my quiet, out of fear I might have to face whatever I am running from? What could the silence and stillness reveal to me? And how the heck will I accomplish all on my to-do list if I take the time to sit in this silence? Before too long, I realize that what I am running from is the very thing that is running me. I think I want to know.

I meditate—for me, meditation often takes the form of quiet time with my books and my writing—to discover the genesis of some angst. What happens then? Is the awareness enough? Enough for what? If I understand the *what* and even the *why* behind what's running me, does it not all bring me back to having to do something about that? I'm not sure I'm on the right track.

The awareness promises some relief. What we can't or won't see easily lurks beneath as a powerful motivator. Being able to name it and claim it gets me out of the dark, as it helps shine a light on what could be the driving force that keeps me wanting to run and hide. And when I get what that is, I might be able to understand myself better and gain a degree of self-compassion. Still, whatever changes I may want to implement have to be accompanied by a stronger motivation, enough to dismantle the one on autopilot. I have to truly want something different. And that's not going to be easy because status quo is what I know. It's my "comfort zone." And we all know how challenging it is to move ourselves out of our comfort zones. That usually only happens when where we *are* is more painful than considering the possibility of an alternative.

Each day I am presented with opportunities to choose, and in that choice I take action. Those actions speak loudly. My inactions do too, and therefore we are not as "hidden" as we believe ourselves to be.

I remember catching my father sitting alone in the dark. As I would enter the blackened space where he sat, sometimes the only visible sign of his presence was his lit cigarette. I would hesitantly approach, but he'd quickly catch me and admit that he was "thinkin' too much." I had to laugh, knowing that he indeed was one who spent hours in thought. Now, as I reflect on those times, I wonder what those thoughts might have been. Were they prayers, talking to God, or were they worries, since he had five children and a wife who chose to live elsewhere? Perhaps he was meditating, listening to God. Either way, he was truly comfortable being by himself, and now I can see how contemplative sitting more easily lends itself to a sort of communion with our oneness. And when I get crazy today with "too much to do," constantly running from here to there without some quiet space, I think of Papa. Whether I wish to talk to God or listen for him, I know that I can do neither when I'm running, but I can do both when I sit alone in the dark.

> The education of the will is the object of our existence.
>
> —Ralph Waldo Emerson

In some way or another, whatever we choose to do as a result of what we want of life requires that we achieve some level of ability to accomplish those desires.

The more we care about what we want, the stronger our desires become, stirring us to act in pursuit. We can move through the learning stages with lightning speed, from not knowing what we don't know to a level of (unconscious) competence—in other words, where our autopilots kick in. Driving a car is a good example; we get from one place to another, often giving little thought to our driving proficiency. Some of our efforts at learning are more deliberate, but we can easily agree that each of us is either teaching or learning all the time, whether or not we are aware of it. And as behavior overrides our words, it is never a matter of if we teach but how and what we teach by our actions. And since we inevitably teach what we ourselves need to learn, the why might be more a matter of "karma."

> Always preach the Gospel and when necessary, use words.
>
> —Saint Francis of Assisi

Doing Work

We judge one another by our professions. When we are doing whatever work we do, others have an idea of the kind of persons we are and what we value. This may provide people with some information about us, but they still may not *know* us.

If we are not doing work that is "ours" to do—meaning work that we love and are destined for, work that was meant for us for one reason or another—we likely are not serving ourselves, let alone the world. And if we somehow are disconnected from our true selves, it may send a message that we do not feel our own sense of worth to pursue the deeper calling of our hearts. The question is, can we be of service to anyone if we are not connected to our authenticity?

> Your work is to discover your work—and then with all your heart to give yourself to it.
>
> —Buddha

In Eastern philosophy, there is a "do what is yours to do" orientation, but that assumes an awareness about what is ours to do. This doesn't have to be interpreted as what we do for a living, necessarily, but it is what we do *in* living. It is more about our responsibility to one another and the overall benefit to humanity in our world.

Spiritual teacher Ram Dass says, "We have to be in the world to learn from it." Our beingness sets us in motion for us to do. The trick is not to get so caught up in the doing that we neglect our responsibility to our own authentic being.

We all know people who seek meaning and fulfillment in their work. They accept nothing less than to live their authentic lives. We consider them fortunate and may even envy them. Some of us wait until midlife to chuck it all and do as we wish. This may involve giving up lots of stuff in the world, stuff that we often come to realize did not make us happy anyway. It is an awareness born of maturity and the ultimate inevitability for us all.

Developmental psychologist Howard Gardner said, "The single most important contribution education can make to a child's development is to help him toward a field where his talents best suit him, where he will be satisfied and competent." This was told to Daniel Goleman, who wrote the book *Emotional Intelligence,* published in 1995, which stimulated a dramatic interest in the subject to this day. Too bad this type of awareness is not part of the education curriculum very early on.

One study confirmed that it is how we feel about what we are doing on the job that matters. We cannot love work to which we are not connected or are not "passionate" about. A finding noted that when people are in jobs for which they are not suited, the effect can be (and likely is) that the workplace evolves into a less emotionally intelligent one; that is, poor morale and employees who are more prone to manifest intolerance on the job. Fortifying this position is a book I read on the Birkman instrument, one of the assessments I work with, which mentioned a case study's conclusion: "To place people in jobs which are characteristically inconsistent with themselves is to guarantee a less emotionally intelligent race."

Placing people in a spot of comfort allows them to be all they can be and to contribute to the world in a way that would be impossible in the opposing circumstance. Yet how many of us are in spots that make little or no sense to us or for us? How many of us live day to day in "quiet desperation," to use Thoreau's words?

How Are You Being in Your Doing?

We may have heard the distinction that we are not human *doings*; we are human *beings*. Even as we do and act and behave and spend an awful lot of time in the activity of our lives, we can't deny our preference to live authentically. If we allow our beingness to do its natural job of informing what we do, we affect our environment of people, places, and things positively.

> Intent is a force that exists in the universe. When sorcerers (those who live of the Source) beckon intent, it comes to them and sets up the path for attainment, which means that sorcerers always accomplish what they set out to do.
>
> —Wayne Dyer

> The master said there is one thing in this world which must never be forgotten. If you were to forget everything else, but were not to forget this, there would be no cause to worry, while if you remembered, performed and attended to everything else, but forgot that one thing, you would in fact have done nothing whatsoever. It is

as if a king had sent you to a country to carry out
one special, specific task. You go to the country
and you perform a hundred other tasks, but if you
have not performed the task you were sent for, it
is as if you have performed nothing at all. So man
has come into the world for a particular task, and
that is his purpose. If he doesn't perform it, he will
have done nothing.

—Sogyal Rinpoche, *The Tibetan
Book of Living and Dying*

We are often distracted from the course we were meant to
pursue. We create these distractions for ourselves in subconscious
self-sabotage. My own example shows that I had gotten
"comfortable" with searching and not having. I kept signing up
for another class, another webinar or workshop; I continued to
read material that told me the same thing in a different way. It
all signifies that I don't have something I need and want and
that I'm still trying to get somewhere. But really, I never will be
satisfied and never will feel fulfilled when I believe myself to be
without. No matter how much material I sign up for, it will never
be enough. There is no end point, no place to "get to."

The red flag here is the wanting and longing. Buddha refers
to this as attachment. I am attached to what I perceive I lack
and will never have, so it's a futile, never-ending search. It is my
personal manifestation of woundedness; we are all wounded

somewhere. But it is a wound of our doing, not in our being, and in that acknowledgement we get to heal.

It is said that our lives are spent trying to get, find, and keep love. It could follow that a great deal of our activity—our doing—has to do with this one compelling drive of humanity.

We still believe that love is somewhere out there. It is a challenge for us to understand that love resides in us and that we don't have to go anywhere to get it. Keeping love, therefore, never could be an issue. We can't get rid of something that is in us and *is* us.

In some of my fondest resources, I've found some helpful teaching that I keep in mind:

- Stop being offended.
- Give up thoughts of harm against others.
- When you feel attacked, don't respond with a counterattack. If you hate the hatred, get angry at the anger—you are using counterforce.
- All conflict is a result that, somewhere in me, I don't feel all right about me.
- Forgiveness is simply letting go.
- Healing is radical, not reasonable.
- Rather than seeking to be informed, seek to be inspired.
- Don't believe there is evil in the world unless you see how you view it to correct something in you. Rather, believe that we are all good people who sometimes do bad things.
- Negative behaviors are the direct outcome of some form

of self-loathing. We cannot feel or do for another what we first do not feel or do for ourselves.

- Rather than praying for something to happen or change, pray for acceptance of what is.
- Consider that there is only love or fear. All negative emotion is fear-based. So when you feel angry or jealous or depressed, ask yourself where the fear is inside you.

Our behavior reflects the ultimate expression of all that preceded it inside us. Recall that behind the behavior is the attitude that created an emotion or feeling about our subject (that often runs us), which came from a belief that originated with a thought. So that by the time we see it in observable behavior, much has taken place. In other words, there are many layers behind it, which means that dismantling it may be a challenge—unless and until, of course, we decide that the pain we experience is too great, and we are ready to welcome relief. Then we are free and likely are able to allow what I call the Holy Spirit—our most accessible Source representative—to enter. We are on our proverbial knees and stand with open hearts, willing to let go and let God. That's when we bring the light into our darkness.

The doing of our lives, for the number of years we are here in any given incarnation, involves "interacting assignments"; in other words, people and places to consider. We have our original family. That extends to friends, on to romantic relationships, and possibly to another family. Then we have work relationships and others. We can see with our eyes that we are not here alone, nor could we do our work without the assistance of other people. We will engage in relationships of all kinds, and this is undoubtedly one of the biggest "doings" of our lives. It is with one another that we work through life circumstances. We don't have relationships; we *do* relationships, and often we do them very poorly, improperly, unfairly, and unappealingly. In fact, this is the arena where we make the greatest blunders of our lives.

The problem is that we cannot do well when we do not see what we are doing, literally and figuratively. Projection is working to keep us in the dark. I see someone or something outside myself as the cause of my unhappiness, but until I recognize my responsibility in the matter, you—the other—will serve me well in my denial of that ownership. One day, when I am willing to see it another way and accept my role in the creation of my life circumstance, I will experience an empowering peace.

Chapter 4

With Whom Will You Do Your Life? Interacting Assignments

If I truly love one person,

I love all persons,

I love the world,

I love life.

If I say to somebody else,

"I love you,"

I must be able to say,

"I love in you everybody,

I love through you the world,

I love in you also myself."

—Erich Fromm

To some extent, if we just follow the logic, the people we collect along the way will depend on what we "decide" we need. That decision determines our actions—*what we choose to do* with those people.

We do not live alone, nor can we. It is inevitable that we need to interact, both in our work lives and at play. There is the romantic relationship and the friendship on one level, the familial on another, our work associations, and then recreation. It's hardly likely, even if we were so inclined, that we would be able to negotiate all life's terrains on our own. Even a consummate introvert will step into relationship somewhere. Besides family associations, they encounter the mailman, the grocery store clerk, or the person with them in the elevator this morning. Here again, we always have choice on how that goes.

Family

We can probably agree that family presents us with our major lessons. *A Course in Miracles* would add "our biggest *forgiveness lessons*" but not in the conventional understanding of the word. Forgiveness, in this context, is letting go of offenses (that never happened anyway).

Who hasn't had their share of struggles on the family front? People have their stories, and I understand that many do not have close ties with their birth families. I believe there are some circumstances in which we can love others without needing to see them or spend time with them. In our worldly forms, we may not be able to put aside our personalities and be in the same space with certain individuals for long periods of time, even if we are connected to them by birth.

To the extent that resolution is avoided, however, we are not quite free to disengage. Endings of relationships in form do not mean that we get to retain our negative feelings or a sense of righteousness. Often, we see that we get to be either right or happy. So we leave our righteousness at the door and retain the love for our "own sake." When a change is decided, we leave the others, keeping our peace and theirs intact. The love goes on, even as the relationship ends in form. It is never finished; love is always. Choosing to love others from across the street instead of in the same room will have to do sometimes.

If we accept that the family into which we are born is purposeful, it behooves us to be at peace with whatever is and learn what there is to learn with them so that we avoid unnecessary and painful repetitions. If there is one certainty, it's that there will be repetition whenever there is no resolution.

I was talking with my older sister one day when I happened to mention the intentional "selection" of our parents.

"Are you telling me that I chose our mother?" she asked. "If you are, I am going to have trouble with that one!"

"Yes," I said, "that is what I am saying."

"Well, I don't think so. I cannot believe that I would actually select her. I mean, we are talking choice here."

"You did, and not only that but you got exactly what you wanted from her."

"Which is to say that I wanted emotional discomfort and chaos?"

"Yes."

"And why would I do that to myself?"

"Because it is what you signed up for. You wanted to learn what only she could teach, and—*voila*—here we all are!"

My sister continued to have trouble with that concept. Every once in a while, when we are having one of our in-depth sister talks, she brings it up. She says that although she now has come to accept that it all might be true, she still has difficulty with the idea that she actually called for such a painful experience. Our mother presented her with the greatest opportunity for getting what she came here for, and so it is appropriate to be grateful for how Mom supplied that precise possibility. It presents my sister with a way to shift the way she held the experience.

Perhaps because I have spent considerable time in discussions with men, I find the relationship of a man to his mother a particularly intriguing one. Two men I knew spoke often and deeply about how their moms made their dads cry and the impact that had on them as young men. This is a dynamic that can prove disastrous for men with the women in their future—both these men had difficult relationships with women in their lives. If we are not careful, if we continue to see victimization instead of responsibility, we can set up defenses based on a past paradigm that has the power to keep us closed off from real love. We will recreate past experiences that play out in our present lives until we acknowledge our roles in creating our circumstances. That key learning is one of the most liberating ... for ourselves and others.

I knew a man who mentioned that his dad "verbally and emotionally abused" his mom. He could not stop visiting the idea that his mom had picked the wrong husband, that she had settled, that they have no business being together, and so on. He flatly rejected the notion of her choice in the matter, making references to "how it was back in the 1940s," when most women married for financial security and did not pursue higher education. Women tended to grow up quickly and leave their homes very young, he said. As an adult, the son had given his mom permission to leave his dad and remained frustrated by her decision to stay, adding the caveat, "if only she had been educated." He could not see that it was never her lack of education that prevented her leaving; it was her willingness to self-inflict pain, at the most, or to be immobilized by guilt, at the very least. Like all negative effects, it all was stimulated by her fear. This is not to blame her but to see that she was not at the effect but rather *the cause* of her life circumstances. Viewing it from that perspective puts us in authentic communication with ourselves. We recognize our choices, enabling us to see how our decisions led to exactly the learning we need to take away from an experience.

Eventually, it is useful to come to an awareness that what happens to us is happening *for* us. We all have had a variety of interesting experiences with the adults in our lives as we were growing up. Our youngest years are significant in that they form our longest-lasting memories, even if they sometimes are "buried alive" in our subconscious minds. We can't underestimate the impact on us as children as we witness the relationship between the two people who are responsible for our births. Few of us can say that what we saw was perfection in the way those two people treated and loved one another or treated and loved us. But like all else in our experiences, we can choose to feel we are victims of circumstance or to see it as it is—two struggling personalities who are doing the best they can with what they have, and all for our benefit. Forgiveness—the letting go of our attachments or opinions about any of it—will serve us (and everyone else along with us) immensely.

Any relationship is purposeful, and it is our own special design for ourselves, from the moment of our arrival to each subsequent encounter and experience while we appear here. Again, we might look to *A Course in Miracles* to simplify: "Every encounter is either an act of love or a call for love." The way we choose to see it determines how quickly we evolve and how we move along from one space to the next, assuming that we move in a forward and upward (positive) direction.

Author Eckhart Tolle writes that life will give us whatever experience is most helpful for the evolution of our consciousness. Whether we acknowledge it or not, we are given what we ask for, what we want, and what we indeed need, and sometimes the "gift" is in the form of a person. It makes perfect sense.

Every relationship and interaction calls on us either to receive the expression of love from another or see his or her behavior as a cry for help. In the light of this acknowledgment, we solve the "problem" of relationship. We actually experience release from the ties that bind us. But until that time, we have a variety of interesting twists and turns around the subject of others in our lives.

After family, we have friends, casual and otherwise. Some of us choose to associate with an intimate few and others of us choose a casual many. This may be dictated by personality preferences and temperament differences, but the adage that we are the company we keep is one that holds weight. The scene is one of symbiosis, with the magnetic pull of *I need you to complete my assignment*. People with whom we have "unfinished business" seem to pop into our lives, pushing a recall button.

Love relationships probably hit us hardest. This artful attraction brings us the one partner (or multiple partners) who may offer harsh lessons under the guise of romantic love. In one way or another, we enter into a perfect dance with a love interest, only to trip and fall and stop and start, all to result in either gaining lessons and getting through the trials or letting go of the relationship. It is a mistake to think that someone else will work better if we have yet to resolve what failed to work with the one before. The other will just be an alternate version of our own issues to force another attempt at resolution or impose a conclusion by parting ways. Our heads will understand it all before our hearts will.

Our "falling in love" is a relationship that is meant to be special; it's the two of you sharing a commitment and a monogamy that binds you together for a time. Of course, it doesn't always work out for all time, but our society recognizes this specialness in traditional marital and legal terms. In some states today, we have invited our homosexual brothers and sisters to join us in this legal stamp of approval and contract.

These commitments are exclusive rather than inclusive, in that we are part of a twosome—no room for any others. Egos can easily use this in a literal way to distance ourselves from loving others. Love is nevertheless universally inclusive. We may retain our worldly form aspects that seem convenient in the life system we have created, but we needn't be hyperactive about the exclusionary terms of our commitment. We reserve certain forms, if we choose, but that is not meant to exclude loving others. Love does not have exclusionary terms and doesn't make one way right and the other way wrong. That is a separation idea that easily causes hurt and assigns blame in not such a healthy way; it is a limited view.

I have long studied relationships and those that fascinate me most are those with an unrequited experience. One person loves another, who fails to return that love in kind. Usually when this occurs, the one left pining may appear without self-esteem intact—lost, sad, perhaps hopelessly depressed.

There are two issues with loving someone who does not return our love. First, that fact alone has nothing to do with our happiness. Or it shouldn't. Second, could we possibly believe that we have only *one chance* at love? That there is but one individual on the planet who is anointed with the label of "love of my life"? I have three myself, and one is a dog, so I don't think so.

Love and romance offer us a variety of growth opportunities, but the largest of these is the idea that there is "the one"—a special someone who will make us happy. That is probably the biggest lie we tell ourselves. It is no one's job to make us happy. Having that expectation will guarantee disappointment.

I remember an *I Love Lucy* episode in which Lucy was convinced that Ricky was cheating on her. In her disappointment, she tells her sidekick, Ethel, "Doesn't eleven years of faithful service count for anything anymore? You'd think if he was going to let me go, he'd give me a gold watch or something." And then she adds the line that causes the ever-certain burst of laughter: "Or a letter of recommendation!"

We really think that someone owes us something for our "service." First, we believe that he or she ought to love us back, and if not, then what do we *get* for the gift of love we bestowed on that person? This attitude signifies a *give-to-get* mind-set that has nothing at all to do with loving anyone or even loving ourselves. It doesn't have anything to do with giving or serving. If this is our attitude, then we need to know that we are neither getting nor giving. It won't yield anything but disappointment, and it's all because we erroneously set up the whole thing in our minds. It isn't even love. Giving to get is conditional and comes from a place of self-protection, born of ideas of scarcity; love is abundant, not scarce.

Some of us refuse to show love, especially when we fear vulnerability in the relationship. Open and authentic expressions of love may leave us open to granting the other an upper hand,

and *we can't have that!* If someone is too sure of our love, we open ourselves up to being taken for granted or losing our freedom. Who knows what that could lead to? These are thought patterns that set us up for superficiality in a relationship and somehow yield a false sense of security in ensuring our safety. One day we may look to the other to blame and criticize him or her for failing to be 100 percent in the relationship, when it is ours alone in projection. We all have our stories.

Some of us find ourselves participating in relationships we call "friendships" when we don't share that level of intimacy to meet the criteria of emotional connection. It makes me think of two women giving a midair kiss in one minute and the vile gossip that follows once they exit each other's space. They fail to be authentic in their communication for fear of losing, fear of being rejected, or fear of conflict. We have all kinds of rationale for this, but the upshot is a superficial relationship, rather than a meaningful one.

> Most of us feel that others will not tolerate such emotional honesty in communication. We would rather defend our dishonesty on the grounds that it might hurt others; and having rationalized our phoniness into nobility, we settle for superficial relationships.
>
> —John Powell, *Why Am I Afraid to Tell You Who I Am?*

The people we have the greatest trouble with are those with whom we have the greatest opportunity. That would mean we potentially have much to gain from those we dislike most. How can we be open to the growth potential offered in these relationships when we can't run fast enough to get far away from these distasteful persons ... and all because they're the "bad guys"?

There ain't no good guys
There ain't no bad guys
There's only you and me
And we just disagree
—Dave Mason, "We Just Disagree"

I remember a line from a sales training class I attended: "When two people want to do business together, the details will never get in the way. When two people do not want to do business together, the details will always get in the way."

I always thought this was the case because people want to like the other before they engage. When they feel good about someone, they go farther, and the mind opens. There is less or no judgment and more acceptance. It is the opposite when the feeling is negative. Then we look for the excuse that will disallow the association to continue.

I remembered that statement because I thought about it so often. In the context of selling, sure, I understood it perfectly well. But the other thing I liked so much about what it says is how it speaks to the possibilities—of the way in which we limit ourselves when we choose fear and how we open ourselves to creative potential when we choose the other way, inferring that anything is possible when we are moved by love.

In the end, our relationship with the other has nothing at all to do with the other and *everything to do with us*. What we know to be true about who we are brings us to a natural recognition of who the other is, thereby allowing for peace and understanding to be the guiding principle and not another story.

"Shooting the messenger" is another analogy for how we project onto another what we need to see in ourselves. We dislike the other in whom we see ourselves, so we shoot the messenger because that is all the other is. It might behoove us to thank the messenger and then heed the message. That way, we have the awareness, and we demonstrate that we no longer need the message. Remember that those messages come in various forms. They range from taps on the shoulder to fatal illnesses.

I was vacationing with a number of friends when the topic of Arabs suddenly entered the conversation. "Why don't sane Arabs stand up and voice their disagreement with the fringe groups who cause all the trouble?" someone asked.

I felt a visceral surge within as I wanted to defend against what I perceived as an attack, albeit benign enough. At minimum, it was a judgment. After another moment, I decided not to choose fear by being defensive and was glad I hadn't reacted.

Later, I reflected on this moment as one in which I had decided not to shoot the messenger, though I wish I'd been able to check in with offering a helpful thought. It is no small wonder why the so-called Middle East crisis has grown to become a world problem. These are a people who have experienced what they view as their land being taken from them. Generation after generation, they have been addicted to crisis. They know nothing else and continue to be offended by something that happened long ago, keeping the past present. They've come to expect the struggle. It's become a national ethos. In other words, it's their story, and they're stickin' to it.

Political attempts at peace treaties haven't worked. The masses are not shifting. Why? For one thing, maybe we are too busy in the story to see another way to help them out of it. Perhaps we ought to ask how we can help them become consciously aware that what they hold on to is a compulsive thought about how they've been "offended." Let's face it; the Mideast crisis has taken on a life of its own. It reminds me of times when two people feud for so long they forget what the fight is about.

Compulsive patterns of thinking keep the battle machine running. Breaking those thought patterns requires replacing them with openness to possibility. Reactive modes of operation preclude creative solutions, as we see in emotional intelligence, which describes the limited options available to us when we cannot think straight. And we are not thinking straight as we fail to be "response-able" and instead resort to compulsive, reactive behaviors. Logic is impotent against the potent energy of reactivity. Perceptual lenses have been clouded; we don't see another way. We can't "solve the problem with the same thinking that created the problem," as Einstein warned. The crisis in the

Middle East needs help to shift the collective thinking. Instead, we're taking sides, joining in the yelling and screaming and prematurely offering peace treaties.

How can there be movement when two groups fight and dig in their self-righteous heels for their polar positions? Perhaps one way is to help them shed their respective victimhood; to accept the fact that they have a choice in the matter. They don't have to feel hurt and be besieged by feelings of resentment and anger. It's only land.

I saw a movie a while back that talked about the usefulness of paradigms because they tell us what is important and what is not. The piece called out for a "paradigm shift" when it becomes obvious that one is necessary, when something no longer works in the way that it had been working. It cited various business-related matters in which companies and countries failed as they continued to operate in an "old paradigm" and were not open to changes that required a shift. I found this a useful concept for the obvious reasons that apply with the Middle East crisis. Yes, each side believes that it is their land, whether God-given or perceived God-given, and this is a crucial matter to the people. But here again, these folks would benefit from a change in thinking that could very well cause the necessary shift to discover workable solutions. And they could do it all without any other country's involvement.

I think that while religion can divide us, spirituality can unite us. That is because man-made religious systems tend to be a separation idea, while spirituality is in all of us, regardless of the religious system of which we choose to be a part.

I love what the Dalai Lama says about his belief in what he calls "a simple religion." It is kindness; he says, "My religion is kindness." Sometimes we overcomplicate what is so very simple, and sometimes simplicity is so difficult for humans. Just imagine a world of relationships where being kind is the order of the day!

Whether in one-on-one relationships or nation to nation, we are united in our humanity, doing life together. The only thing in the way of our peace and joy are thoughts of separation. Somewhere, we all know this.

Chapter 5

How Long Will You Stay? Duration in Time

We are terrified of our appointment with Death.

—Wayne Dyer

What length of time are you signed on for ... this time? (That is, if you believe in this time versus last time and next time.) Some of us make grand entrances; others make dramatic exits. What accounts for the differences? Do we choose our entrance and exit, and if so, what do you choose for yourself?

I have often wondered about the mystery of the number of days we appear here and how it all comes to a close. One explanation is that this experience is a forgiveness lesson; we are here until we learn forgiveness or at least inspire it in others. But people certainly seem to die without having had the experience of forgiveness. Just think of the recent examples of those who kill several people at one time and subsequently turn the killing weapon on themselves. It appears the killers chose to leave violently and in a mode of hatred, not forgiveness, whether we use the conventional definition of forgiveness or not. Those perpetrators neither forgave others for what they thought others did to hurt them, nor did they shift their perceptions. It was their attachment, more than anything, that led them to take out their hurt on innocent others. They projected and acted on those projections. Perhaps their purpose was to remind us of our love and compassion, given the human bonding that tends to occur in the aftermath of such unconscionable incidents.

What if it is true that each of us arrives with some knowledge of exactly why we came in and exactly when we will depart our earthy experience? Our conscious selves do not recall this useful information, but deep in our souls, hidden in some private spot where we had our meeting with God, is the answer. It cannot matter because it doesn't change anything, and to be sure, conscious awareness of this fact might be unnerving. We come in, we go out, and in the middle is a tiny space we call time, where we experience the dream of a lifetime. In this theory I personally experience my greatest relief and receptivity.

We stay until we have satisfied the reason for our visit in the first place. It is both to learn and to teach. The content is the same, but we each have a unique form. That is generally our purpose; the form appears to be different for each of us, and that includes what we know as the "number of years." In some cases, it is so brief that it causes more sadness than joy, and the huge question that seems to linger is *why?*

One of the best books I've read on exploring the "reasons" for the passing of a young child was Rabbi Harold Kushner's *When Bad Things Happen to Good People*. In it, Kushner reacts to the unspeakable personal loss of his young adolescent child to the horrifying disease that causes premature aging, progeria. What he came to understand about that loss, after questioning God for some time, was that God is not involved in the details of our human existence. Things happen in our form circumstance, and there is nothing personal about those circumstances. It is Kushner's belief that God neither causes nor prevents suffering, so there is no "making sense" of any of it. There is a randomness at work, and our job is simply to forgive the world (of our making) for not being perfect.

I heard Dr. Brian L. Weiss, the author of *Many Lives, Many Masters*, speak of his explorative journey with one of his patients, during which time he became convinced of reincarnation in the human experience. Referencing the death of his own child, this renowned psychiatrist reflected back and saw that his child's life was meant to teach him one of his greatest lessons. I can categorize that lesson as forgiveness, but that's only because it appears to all come down to letting go—for others and, ultimately, for ourselves.

We gain from whatever lesson is presented so as to avoid the need to repeat it, particularly those that are immensely painful. It will re-present itself until we have accepted the learning. It is possible that we may not recognize it next time because of the likelihood that the lesson will be disguised in an alternate form circumstance, which could delay progress awhile. Still, we will get it when we are ready; we know that timing is an individual choice.

My father stayed for eightysomething years (we had no exact date for his birth). In that number of years, it seemed he lived a full and good life. I never knew him when he was young, but from what he told us, his youth was eventful and exciting and somewhat terrifying in some ways on some days. Still, he advanced through life, making it to maturity, happily responsible for his five children in a country other than his native home. He was exceedingly strict and hardworking. It was a life.

Once, not so long before his body gave out, I rushed over to his home in a panic about his feverish condition. The moment I opened the door, I was stunned when he greeted me by sitting up on his bed and announcing with great confidence that he was "not ready yet." He had his index finger pointing upward and mentioned something about how *Allah knows*. To me, it seemed like he had a date in mind, and only he and God—Allah—were privy to it. The postponement was okay with me. I was never going to be ready for him to leave.

When he decided to go, it was a quiet exit. I rationalized that he must have been ready. His children were all adults by then, and he had two grandsons by his only son, which meant that his name would live on. I thought and still think that those two boys are a fitting tribute to his legacy.

And so, what was the purpose of this life of a man we very affectionately called Papa? He came from a rural village in Yemen and spoke of a farm and sheep and of a stepmom he casually referenced as holding no great love for him. He struggled and was adventurous in leaving his country at a rather young age, going on to England. He worked on a ship, perhaps more than one, which allowed him to see many places and other countries, until he decided to land in New York City sometime in the 1940s. Through connections, mostly with other Arabs, he made his way to the western part of the state to work as a steel plant laborer and ended up raising his family there.

I have experienced his life mentally, as a theatrical production, as well as the lives of others who have transitioned. I see that each moment in a person's life serves to advance him or her toward a particular end goal. Each of those segments of time were indeed tiny pieces of a puzzle that somehow fit together to tell a certain story, one with a moral to it and that leaves people affected by it.

From where I stood, I could have had no other father. And for his example, I understand that five times over, since he successfully raised five children. His sphere of influence is much greater once you add his wife (our mother) and all the folks with whom he engaged for all the years he was here, traveling through time.

It seems that we all are created equal and perfect, but we forget that upon our earthly birth and enter into situations that mold our experiences. These create a unique set of circumstances, and we will choose to respond to them in ways that will allow our distinctive histories. If we fail to see this as our own creation, we will feel victimized by it.

Consider the "visit" you signed on for this time. Do you think that you have been here before, having experienced déjà vu in places and moments of your life? Would you agree that these lifetimes are cumulative, that your mind is holographic and thus contains the learning of the previous lifetimes each time? If this is true, are all these incarnations predetermined, or do you have a say in influencing the number of visits here? How far along in your evolution are you this time around? Is it helpful to investigate these questions, or are they better left unconsidered?

There is a belief that we tend to sign on with the same people. The combination of energy produced by those relationships is necessary to our own growth and evolution. So consider with whom you signed on and for what purpose you were brought together, perhaps more than once.

I recently listened to a speech by a man who had been given a death sentence from his illness, and he knew approximately when death could come. He chose to travel to groups to give talks and sage advice. I wonder how many of us could do that.

I was moved, hearing him speak so eloquently about what he wanted to leave us with, given what he knew, as he had his "end date" in mind. I wondered if we were only temporarily moved. Could we really hear this man's words? Did we need to be in his position to understand the power and meaning of his words?

After my father's trauma of retirement, he settled into a different calm presence, one that was aware that time had passed. It seemed he was almost preparing to leave us, to pass the family torch. Initially, he had kicked and screamed his way to retirement, still seeming to be attached to his ability to earn a living. I came to understand that he did not mourn the loss of the job as much as he did the loss of the associations he had so successfully cultivated—the friendships and camaraderie. Papa loved people.

Just as we chose our births, the people to whom we were born, and all the circumstances that are to cause our desired experience, we also may choose our deaths.

How will you leave? Will you go quietly into the night, your body no longer visible in the world, or will you suffer much before it ends? Will you choose a particular wake-up call in the form of illness, or do you have a smoother and kinder way to be awakened from your slumber?

You may see how you set up an illness, so then you can work on it. You can will yourself to not have the disease, or you can surrender to it. My friend Christine was diagnosed with a malignant brain tumor. She told me that she understood why she was given this fate; love and attention was what she sought throughout her life and was angry that love eluded her. She said she would fight this with all she had. I believed her, so when she left soon after this claim, I was deeply affected. Is it not better to get out of the battleground and forgive, to let go of our resentments? I wish we would stop using the language of war with our sickness and disease.

According to New Age thinking, the word *disease* is really "not at ease." How are you not at ease? What have you not let go of? What are you still attached to? Sickness is thought to be a fear of awakening, but what are we afraid of knowing?

Someone asked Confucius, "What surprises you most about mankind?"

Confucius answered,

> They lose their health to make money and then lose money to restore their health. By thinking anxiously about the future, they forget the present, such that they live neither for the present nor the future and they live as if they will never die, and they die as if they had never lived.

I remember being at the deathbed of someone for whom I cared dearly, and I found myself repeating the phrase, "You are love; remember that." I knew that it was for me that I was remembering in that moment, in union with my "someone else."

I never quite understood the idea that God gives us only what we can handle. It does not seem to be true. First, there were people seemingly having great difficulty with their unique form of challenge; and second, is God actually giving illness to us? It makes more sense to me that it is our own choosing. I know that God creates only perfection, so how can he dole out our personal challenges if he did not make them and wouldn't wish them for us? Would he even recognize that we have this thing to handle if he sees only the perfection that we are, as he created us?

We can ask ourselves what we are getting out of this. What is our investment in this challenge?

If an illness is another opportunity to wake up, then how can we shed our injurious attitudes to welcome health back into our lives?

Ram Dass says in *Still Here*, "Healing does not mean going back to the way things were before, but rather allowing what is now to move us closer to God." He speaks of philosophical materialism, "the idea that reality is limited by what we perceive through our senses."

We don't want cures, he says; they restore us to a past condition. We want healing, using what is here to move us deeply to soul awareness. And, reminding us of our emotional intelligence, he reemphasizes that avoiding our fears only feeds them.

The links between our emotional state and our physical well-being (the mind/body connection) has long been established. For example, we know that the sympathetic nervous system, which stimulates our fight-or-flight response, activates adrenal glands that release hormones into the bloodstream, which causes the body to speed up and become more tense. Blood pressure increases. This state remains in the body for forty-five minutes to an hour. Imagine being stressed out multiple times a week or even days and the cumulative effect that has on your physical health. We need to consider the value of dropping all those judgments of self and others that wreak havoc in our minds and bodies.

Chronic stress secretes cortisol into the bloodstream and lasts hours, ultimately affecting our immune systems. Attack thoughts in the mind, usually unconscious, may become symbolized by the body attacking itself, as with cancer.

During periods of increased stress, "the immune cells are

being bathed in molecules which are essentially telling them to stop fighting," according to Dr. Esther Sternberg (*Today's Dietician*, 20). These molecules, namely cortisol, suppress the immune system and inflammatory pathways, rendering the body more susceptible to disease.

Do You Believe in Magic?

I remember when I read in *A Course in Miracles* a reference to Western medicine as a belief in magic. I recognized that very notion as one that was at home in me, prior to having read it there. It was as if I'd written those words and sung that tune and was, at that moment, gratified to hear it as validation of what I already knew or at least suspected. I barely could be talked into taking an aspirin when I had a headache or as a remedy when I had flulike symptoms. My parents were the same way, as are my siblings, so I just considered it a family ethos. Reading it in *A Course in Miracles* and knowing that these words came from Jesus simply created a space for embracing the truth-- of all humankind in our oneness as God's children, impervious to sickness, even when it appears that the body is otherwise engaged.

We spend fortunes to support our cover stories, rather than address the underlying causation of how an illness was developed and sustained. We are better advised to look into where it occurs instead of reacting in unconscious terror. Every challenge presents a growth opportunity, even if and when we require a little magic.

I love our metaphorical language associated with waking up

or remaining in a less than conscious state. We use the term *wake up* when we wish to convey a sense of urgency to have someone get something. We say "He is in the dark about that," and "She saw the light," or "It dawned on me." Moving into consciousness may not restore us to our past conditions but *we will heal.*

> The world is not left by death but by truth.
>
> —*A Course in Miracles*

So how shall you stay on while you're here, and will you return for unfinished business?

Our thoughts are like negatives in a camera. Every time you expose a negative to the light, it weakens the image until, eventually, the image is no longer visible.

By bringing awareness to your old thought patterns or autopilot behavior, you weaken them. As you continue to weaken those habitual, old, and damaging thought patterns, you replace them with only what is true—love. Forget the resentment; replace it with love and forgiveness.

On Criticism

When you stop short of criticizing another, other people automatically will feel better in your presence.

When you adopt the belief that anything others say about you is only their opinion, you cannot be offended or hurt.

Have a mind that is open to everything and attached to nothing.

Although you can't change what happens, you always can change your mind.

Recognize that your decisions reflect how you feel, and your feelings come from your attitudes, which originated in your belief that came from a thought.

Thoughts have energy, and what you think about expands; what you resist, persists.

Consider the words of Oscar Wilde, "Criticism is the only reliable form of autobiography."

How Long Is Your Stay?

I love the not-so-little blue book, *A Course in Miracles*. It has helped me, along with countless others, shed light on those mysteries of living here. It has brought us out of darkness and into light. It has simplified and demystified the meaning of living and dying. It has delivered great personal peace, even as its claim is that it is only one way, not *the* way.

> Here the world of idols has been set by the idea this power and place and time are given form, and shape the world where the impossible has happened. Here the deathless come to die, the all-encompassing to suffer loss, the timeless to be made the slaves of time. Here does the changeless change; the peace of God, forever given to all living things, give way to chaos. And the Son of God, as

perfect, sinless and as loving as his Father, come to hate a little while; to suffer pain and finally to die.

—*A Course in Miracles*, T-29.VIII.7

There are universal lessons, like separation and forgiveness. There is only fear or love. We may learn and then teach, or we may not be here long enough, as in the early departure of a child or baby. Then it would appear to be a teaching-only assignment. There is karma. Waking from the dream will require wrapping our heads around an obtuse concept.

They seem to lose what they love, perhaps the most insane belief of all.

—*A Course in Miracles*, p. 220

Chapter 6

Coming Full Circle
Life's Ultimate
Meaning

The word "belief" is a difficult thing for me. I
don't believe. I must have a reason for a certain
hypothesis. Either I know a thing, and then I know
it—I don't need to believe it.
              —Carl Jung (1875–1961),
                            Swiss psychiatrist

Jung's words resonated with me. It got me thinking about what
I believe and what I know—or think I know. Part of *Webster's
Dictionary* definition of the word *know* includes "to recognize
as being the same as something previously known ... to be
convinced or certain of ... to have a practical understanding
of ..." The word *believe* is defined as "to have a firm religious

faith ... to accept something as true, genuine, or real." Knowing bypasses belief.

We all know we are going to die because there is evidence and undeniable proof that we, as members of the human race, will one day cease to have a bodily presence on this planet. But we part company when it comes to our beliefs about what happens following our physical deaths. Even though there seems to be evidence from near-death experiences, we cannot know for certain what will be until we get there. That's why we have a variety of beliefs, aligned with nonsecular and secular thought. Meaning and purpose of our time here may be aligned in a similar fashion.

After we have questioned who we are, what we want here, how we take action with the desires of our lives, and with whom we shall spend this so-called time we have signed on for, it all comes to an inevitable conclusion. So what will it all have meant?

Of course, there are those among us who suggest that our time here means absolutely nothing; it's all an evolutionary conundrum. Earlier in this writing, I inferred how it just may be that these same people secretly hold one eye open to the other possibility.

I was watching a PBS special on the world-renown anthropologist Jane Goodall, who has made a major contribution in the study of chimpanzees in East Africa. Journalist Bill Moyers was probing this subject of meaning when Ms. Goodall responded that she just understood without having to ask why. She said that maybe we ask too often, and maybe we should just be satisfied with *the knowing.* She spoke of being comfortable with mystery and noted that faith cannot be scientifically explained. She spoke of her own mother giving her the encouragement to do what she loved. She unequivocally gave credit to her mom, who saw "no conflict" in the relationship between religion and evolution. Somewhere near the conclusion of the interview, Mr. Moyers asked Ms. Goodall to read a poem that she wrote called "The Old Wisdom." In it, she calls out to "the Eternal I." Here is one verse:

Yes, my child, go out into the world; walk slow
And silent, comprehending all, and by and by
Your soul, the Universe, will know
Itself: the Eternal I.

Legacy

If we care about what others think of us after we leave our bodies, we must be concerned with legacy. What do we leave behind with those we love and as a memento of our time here? What did we affect? How so?

It may be oversimplifying to say that if you contributed positively to your earthly environment for however long you're here, it is a life well lived. If you failed to contribute or if you, in fact, detracted from your environment in ways that injured yourself and others, then perhaps it signals a need to return for another chance, with another life, to set things right. It's a thought.

There is a line in one of my favorite church hymns, "All I ask of you is forever to remember me as loving you." It always makes me sad to hear it, as it is sometimes sung at funeral masses, but I do love the message. We all need to know that we are loved. In the end, what else is there? What better feeling is there than having been loved? How would it be if we could always remember that we are loved? That we *are* love?

A lot was made of Apple cofounder Steve Jobs's final word, "Wow," which he was said to have uttered three times as he left his body. Why are we intrigued by that? Might it be the suggestion of the possible wonder to come, that same wonder that we question while here in our bodies? Is it made all the more profound because it came from the mouth of someone we would not associate with such metaphysical acknowledgment?

We might need to consider that Jobs was experiencing an "awakening," even as he was seeming to leave us by leaving his body. Jesus assures us in *A Course in Miracles* that an awakening experience is for all; it is only a matter of what we know as *time*.

> Is it possible for anyone to get enlightened in this lifetime? The state is already there; it only needs to be awakened.
>
> —Baba Hari Dass

Meaning of Life from the Death of Those We Love

I started this little project admitting that this was not about answers to our most profound queries about life. It was more about how we are joined in this experience of questioning the meaning of our time here. Facing this final chapter allowed me to consider that I may have something more specific to add about life's purpose. I have the perspective of one who has loved and lost, not unlike many of you. And even as I write that, I know that although it is how we phrase it, we have not lost those we love. They are still with us; they live in our hearts and have become part of how we have evolved to this minute.

What can we offer from the love we shared with departed loved ones in response to the question of the meaning of life? We know that our worth is easily reflected back to us in our relationships. In fact, the others in our lives reflect back to us all we need to know of ourselves, clearly providing hints of life's meaning. What is left behind is etched in memory for our forever benefit.

It is said that we learn what love is and how to love from our earliest experiences. It is also said that by the time we reach the age of three to seven years, we have our personality for life. If certain personality characteristics remain fairly consistent throughout our lifetimes, it suggests the critical importance of our earliest years and how we are cared for and loved. What follows are myriad experiences that either reinforce those traits or possibly modify them.

My own experiences in this way shaped me for the better. My parents definitely were able to transfer a love to me that allowed me to feel secure and content. Even though they were not always together, I saw a mutual love and respect, for the most part, which may have led me to have an easy time with loving and respecting myself and others. Both my parents loved their children and demonstrated a kindness toward one another.

The meaning of my parents' lives had to in part have been to give life and love to their five offspring and ultimately affect the 41 spirits having a human experience just because of their union. I personally am in awe of what can happen when two people join together to contribute to the world!

From my dear departed friend, I learned so much, bringing me to consider life's meaning in terms of the abundance one can teach in a brief amount of time. For one, I learned empathy and pure, unadulterated acceptance. My forgiveness capacity was tested, yet in the end, I understood that there was never anything to forgive. It enabled me to let go of the idea of being offended. The entire experience was a strong reminder (I had forgotten) of what love calls on us to do. I saw that what we so often try to call love is really not love at all but rather control and possession, rising out of fear. I acquired a clear understanding of giving to get versus giving without attachment. I came to appreciate those distinctions more than I could have ever anticipated when I was in the middle of it.

I also came into a clear understanding of the profound connection between the devastating fear of loss and the genesis of manipulative and controlling behaviors. I learned of the polar concepts of scarcity and abundance; that on one end there will never be enough versus the quiet comfort derived from an abundance orientation.

I knew fun and laughter and what happens when two lost

souls are brought together to enjoy a worldly experience. I saw how two people can help one another overcome their fears and join in holding up the light for the other to see. I felt the pain of loss at such a deep soul level that taught me how much a life could mean. I learned how I could conquer all kinds of fears, propelled by the power of love.

And from a small and absolutely beautiful twelve-pound white-haired four-legged being with big black eyes, how could I have ever guessed what his life would come to mean to me in sixteen and a half years? He taught me the greatest awareness and love of all animals, something I doubt ever would have been possible without him. He communicated patience and service at the deepest level, seriously instructing me on both. I would have had it no other way. I am reminded of a quote by novelist and poet Anatole France: "Until one has loved an animal, a part of one's soul remains unawakened."

We are in no short supply of beliefs and theories about our time here and what it means, most of which have their basis in religion. The problem with organized religion is that it has to be "managed" by fallible humans, and there is no shortage of screw-ups there. That's why people assure us that there is a difference between *spiritual* and *religious*. Unfortunately, it seems these can be mutually exclusive orientations.

Author and rabbi Harold Kushner wrote, "The need for meaning is not a biological need like the need for food and air. Neither is it a psychological need, like the need for acceptance and self-esteem [referencing Maslow's hierarchy of needs]." He says that the quest for life's meaning is a religious need, which he refers to as "an ultimate thirst of our souls." (*When All You've Ever Wanted Isn't Enough: The Search for A Life that Matters*)

In *A Course in Miracles*, Jesus says that the world is not left by death but by truth. I understand that to mean that while there is no death, per se, the truth of who we are sets us free of this world of our making—or in Jesus's terms, our "own nightmare."

There is no death because we are not bodies, although we seem to have bodies that we use while we are here in our dream universe. But we can leave here with an acknowledgment that where we really are is at home, safe in God's kingdom, making separation only a figment of our imaginations.

I am certain of this much: Our seeming time here could never derive any meaning from what we accumulate, how we look, or even what we do. In fact, it could never have anything to do with our bodies and what we spend so much time on. Whether we understand that on our "way out" or in a subsequent try at another lifetime, we will get it and find our way home.

No one believes there really was a time when he knew nothing of a body, and could never have conceived this world as real.

—*A Course in Miracles*, T-27.VIII.5:5

Printed in the United States
By Bookmasters